SOTHEBY'S
ART AT AUCTION 1986– 87

A Byzantine mosaic originally from the church of Santa Maria Assunta, Torcello, *circa* 1070,
height 18½in (47cm)
London £264,000 ($432,960). 9.VII.87

SOTHEBY'S
ART AT AUCTION 1986–87

SOTHEBY'S PUBLICATIONS

© Sotheby's 1987

First published for Sotheby's Publications by
Philip Wilson Publishers Ltd,
26 Litchfield Street, London WC2H 9NJ
and
Sotheby's Publications,
Harper & Row, Publishers, Inc.,
10 East 53rd Street, New York, NY 10022

ISBN 0 85667 342 0
ISSN 0084–6783
Library of Congress Catalog Card Number 67 30652

Editor: Georgia Fogg
Assistant Editors: Sally Liddell (London); Elizabeth White (New York)
Assistants: Tessa Kennedy (London); Laurel Colvin (New York)

Design: Liz Jobling
Printed in England by Jolly & Barber Ltd, Rugby, Warwickshire,
and bound by Dorstel Press Ltd, Harlow, Essex

Note
Prices given throughout this book include the buyer's premium applicable in the saleroom concerned.
These prices are shown in the currency in which they were realized. The sterling and dollar
equivalent figures, shown in brackets, are based on the rates of exchange on the day of sale.

Sotheby's galleries at Bond Street, Bloomfield Place and Conduit Street are indicated by the
designation 'London', and those at York Avenue by the designation 'New York'.

Endpapers
A documentary 'Stein Kabinett' by Christian Friedrich Neuber, Dresden, *circa* 1795,
width $6\frac{7}{8}$in (17.5cm)
Geneva SF99,000 (£41,949:$60,366). 13.XI.86

Contents

A jadeite box and cover in the form of an archaic bronze vessel, height 5½in (14cm)
Hong Kong HK$2,090,000(£161,017:$267,949). 19.V.87
From the T.Y. Chao private and family trust collections

Preface

A. Alfred Taubman
Chairman, Sotheby's Holdings, Inc.

This edition of *Art at Auction* records the events of the most successful year in our history. In our 243rd year of operation, Sotheby's captured better than sixty percent of the international auction market, for the first time surpassing one billion dollars in sales. No other art auction house has reached this historic milestone.

The objects offered in our salerooms were of exceptional quality. Among the year's triumphs were the sales of the John R. Gaines collection of Old Master and modern drawings, the Scull collections of Contemporary art, the T.Y. Chao Collections of Chinese art, botanical colour-plate books from the celebrated library of Robert de Belder, paintings from the collection of Caroline Ryan Foulke and the Old Master Print Collection of the British Rail Pension Funds. And, of course, the April sale of the Duchess of Windsor's jewels captured the world's attention.

The season's dramatic increase in the participation of collectors reflects the breadth of Sotheby's client services. We have broadened our financial services and strengthened our international network, simplifying procedures to help collectors participate in auctions all over the world. Our educational programs have been expanded in both the United Kingdom and the United States. In addition, Sotheby's publications continue to provide collectors with important international resources.

As part of an ongoing program to improve our facilities, we completed extensive restoration and renovation of our offices and galleries in London. This work will enhance the working environment, while maintaining the building's unique historic character. In New York, we returned the world headquarters of Sotheby's International Realty to Madison Avenue from its suburban location in Greenwich, Connecticut.

Recognizing the year's outstanding achievements, I congratulate, on behalf of the Board of Directors, Sotheby's senior management team: Michael L. Ainslie, President and Chief Executive Officer, Sotheby's Holdings Inc.; The Rt. Hon. The Earl of Gowrie, Chairman, and Timothy D. Lewellyn, Managing Director of Sotheby's United Kingdom; Julian Thompson, Chairman, and Simon de Pury, Managing Director, Sotheby's International; and John L. Marion, Chairman, and Diana D. Brooks, President, Sotheby's North America.

Baccio della Porta, called Fra Bartolommeo
THE VIRGIN AND CHILD CROWNED BY TWO ANGELS, WITH THREE OTHER
ANGELS PRESENTING A KNEELING MONASTIC SAINT AND THE INFANT ST JOHN;
ABOVE, A SEPARATE STUDY FOR ONE OF THE ANGELS
Pen and brown ink heightened with white on paper washed pink,
8¾in by 6in (22.4cm by 15.4cm)
New York $440,000 (£307,692). 17.XI.86
From the collection of John R. Gaines

On the reverse is a drawing in pen and brown ink heightened with white of
an angel kneeling.

Paintings and drawings

Lorenzo Monaco
THE PROPHET ISAIAH
Tempera on panel, inscribed on the scroll *ECCE VIRGO CON CIP*, diameter 7⅝in (19.5cm)
London £275,000 ($451,000). 8.VII.87

The roundel is the missing element from the upper part of the right wing of the *Annunciation* triptych painted by Lorenzo Monaco, *circa* 1409, for the Florentine church of San Procolo.

Domeniko Theotokopoulos, called El Greco
CRISTO CON LA CRUZ A CUESTAS
Signed, *circa* 1585–90, 26⅜in by 19⅞in (67cm by 50.5cm)
Madrid Ptas93,020,800 (£467,441: $721,091). 17.III.87

Sebastiano Ricci
THE PATIENCE OF JOB
37in by 45⅝in (94cm by 116cm)
London £104,500 ($155,705). 10.XII.86

Opposite
Rembrandt Harmensz. van Rijn
PORTRAIT OF A GIRL, WEARING A GOLD-TRIMMED CLOAK
On panel, signed and dated *1632*, 23¼in by 17¼in (59cm by 44cm)
London £7,260,000 ($10,817,400). 10.XII.86
From the collection of the family of Robert Treat Paine, II

Pier Francesco Cittadini
INTERIEUR AVEC VASES DE FLEURS, INSTRUMENTS DE MUSIQUE ET OISEAUX
65in by 93¼in (165cm by 237cm)
Monte Carlo FF999,000 (£107,419: $153,692). 29.XI.86

Opposite
Monogrammist I.F.
JEUNE SERVANTE DEVANT UNE TABLE DE CUISINE
On panel, signed with monogram and dated *1635*, 45¼in by 33½in (115cm by 85cm)
Monte Carlo FF2,331,000 (£233,100: $388,500). 20.VI.87

Pieter Breughel, the Younger
PEASANTS EATING AND DRINKING OUTSIDE A VILLAGE INN
On panel, signed and dated *1632*, 19½in by 28½in (49.5cm by 72.5cm)
New York $495,000 (£303,681). 4.VI.87

Opposite
Jan van Huysum
STILL LIFE OF FLOWERS IN A VASE ON A MARBLE LEDGE
Signed, 29¼in by 21½in (74.4cm by 54.6cm)
New York $396,000 (£242,945). 4.VI.87
From the collection of the Kimbell Art Foundation, Fort Worth, Texas

Jean-Baptiste Oudry
AN ALLEGORY OF EUROPE
Signed and dated *1722*, 63¾in by 59¾in (162cm by 152cm)

Jean-Baptiste Oudry
AN ALLEGORY OF ASIA
Signed, 63¾in by 59¾in (162cm by 152cm)

This pair of paintings was sold in London on 8 July 1987 for £418,000 ($685,520). They form part of a set of four allegories of the continents; those representing *Africa* and *America* are at Versailles and are similarly signed and dated 1722.

Bernardo Strozzi called Il Cappuccino
AN ALLEGORY OF CHARITY
50¾in by 43¾in (129cm by 111cm)
London £473,000 ($775,720). 8.VII.87

Pompeo Girolamo Batoni
PORTRAIT OF THE RT REV., THE HON. FREDERICK AUGUSTUS HERVEY, BISHOP OF DERRY,
LATER 4TH EARL OF BRISTOL
Signed and dated *1778*,
68⅛in by 39¾in (173cm by 101cm)
London £231,000 ($390,390). 8.IV.87

François Boucher
A BOY WITH A GIRL BLOWING BUBBLES
Signed, 40in by 49¼in (101.5cm by 125cm)
New York $1,925,000 (£1,283,333). 15.I.87
From the Patiño collection

Opposite
François Boucher
LE SOMMEIL DE VENUS
Signed and dated *1754*, 40⅜in by 35½in (102.5cm by 90cm)
Monte Carlo FF4,440,000 (£473,118:$676,923). 29.XI.86
From the collection of the late Countess Mona Bismarck

Fig. 1
Leonardo da Vinci
SHEET OF STUDIES, INCLUDING THREE SKETCHES OF A CHILD EMBRACING A LAMB
Black chalk and pen and brown ink, inscribed with three lines of text in mirror
writing, *circa* 1503–1506, 8in by 5⅜in (20.3cm by 13.8cm)
New York $3,630,000 (£2,538,462). 17.XI.86

This drawing is now in the collection of the J. Paul Getty Museum, Malibu,
California. On the reverse is a sheet of studies: a child with a lamb, the head
of an old man, studies of machinery and several lines of explanatory text in
mirror writing.

Fig. 2
Rembrandt Harmensz. van Rijn
VIEW OF HOUTEWAAL NEAR THE SINT ANTHONISPOORT
Pen and brown ink and grey-brown wash with bodycolour, *circa* 1650,
5in by 7¼in (12.6cm by 18.3cm)
New York $957,000 (£669,231). 17.XI.86

The drawing is illustrated actual size. On the reverse is a pen and brown ink study of *Figures on the Anthonisdijk entering Houtewaal from the west*.

Fig. 3
Edgar Degas
LE PAS BATTU
Pastel over monotype in black ink on laid paper, signed, *circa* 1879,
$10\frac{5}{8}$in by $11\frac{5}{8}$in (27cm by 29.5cm)
New York $1,100,000 (£769,231). 17.XI.86

Agostino Carracci
THE LAST SUPPER
Pen and brown ink and wash over black chalk, 10⅜in by 14in (26.5cm by 35.5cm)
Monte Carlo FF888,000 (£89,788: $146,293). 20.VI.87
From the collection of Michel Gaud

Opposite
Pieter Coecke van Aelst
SCENES FROM THE LIFE OF THE PRODIGAL SON
Pen and brown ink and grey wash over black chalk, 7½in by 20¼in (19cm by 51.3cm)
Amsterdam DFl207,000 (£64,688: $92,825). 1.XII.86

Andrea del Sarto
THE HEAD OF SAINT JOHN THE BAPTIST
Black chalk on paper laid down on panel,
12¾in by 9¼in (32.5cm by 23.3cm)
New York $165,000 (£110,000). 14.I.87

Taddeo Zuccaro
STUDY OF A SEATED MALE NUDE
Black chalk with touches of white chalk on blue paper, 9¼in by 7⅛in (23.4cm by 18cm)
Monte Carlo FF532,800 (£53,873:$87,776). 20.VI.87
From the collection of Michel Gaud

On the reverse is a study of three figures in black chalk, heightened with white, a preparatory study for Taddeo's fresco of *The Last Supper* in Santa Maria della Consolazione, Rome, 1556.

Andrea Boscoli
HEAD OF A YOUTH, SEEN FROM ABOVE
Red and black chalk, $11\frac{1}{4}$in by $8\frac{1}{2}$in (28.6cm by 21.5cm)
Monte Carlo FF310,800 (£31,426: $51,203). 20.VI.87
From the collection of Michel Gaud

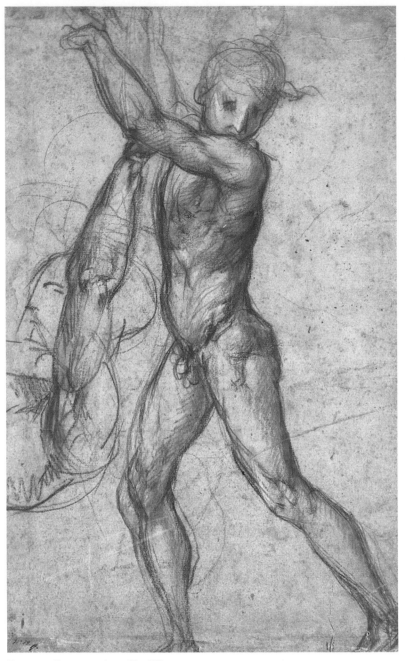

Jacopo Carrucci, called Pontormo
STUDY OF A STANDING MALE NUDE, AND PART OF ANOTHER NUDE FIGURE
Red chalk with touches of white chalk, 15¼in by 9½in (38.8cm by 24cm)
London £352,000 ($577,280). 6.VII.87

On the reverse is a red chalk study of a seated male nude, a further
preparatory study for Pontormo's altarpiece of 1518 in S. Michele
Visdomini, Florence.

Laurent de la Hyre
THE RAPE OF EUROPA
Black chalk with touches of grey wash heightened with white, 14½in by 11⅜in
(36.8cm by 29cm)
New York $29,700 (£19,800). 14.I.87

Jan van der Straet, called Stradanus
CHASSEURS OFFRANT DES OISEAUX A UNE DAME DE QUALITE
Pen and brown ink and blue wash on blue paper, signed *Strada*, $7\frac{7}{8}$in by $11\frac{7}{8}$in (20cm by 30.2cm)
Monte Carlo FF333,000 (£36,156: $55,152). 1.III.87
From the collection of the late Marcel Jeanson

One of twenty-five drawings by Stradanus, which were made in preparation for engravings
published by Philippe Gallé in Antwerp before 1596, as part of the series entitled *Venationes Ferarum
Auium Piscium . . .*

Giuseppe Cesari, called Cavalier d'Arpino
HEAD OF A SATYR
Black and red chalk, 8¼in by 7⅝in (21cm by 19.5cm)
London £4,620 ($7,346). 19.II.87
From the collection of the late Sir John and Lady Witt

This drawing is probably a preparatory study for the frieze above the fresco *The Rediscovery of the She-Wolf*, 1596–97, in the Palazzo dei Conservatori, Rome.

Jean-Honoré Fragonard
INTERIOR OF A PARK: THE GARDENS OF THE VILLA D'ESTE
Gouache on vellum, $7\frac{7}{8}$in by $9\frac{5}{8}$in (19.9cm by 24.4cm)
New York $203,500 (£135,667). 14.I.87

This a reduced version of Fragonard's painting of the same subject, *circa* 1763–65, now in the
Wallace Collection, London.

Opposite
François Boucher
YOUNG GIRL RECLINING
Red and white chalk over black chalk underdrawing, $12\frac{3}{8}$in by $18\frac{1}{8}$in (31.6cm by 46.2cm)
London £286,000 ($469,040). 6.VII.87
From the collection of the Kimbell Art Foundation, Fort Worth, Texas

This is a preparatory study for Boucher's painting *The Dark-haired Odalisque*, *circa* 1743, said to be
the Irish beauty Miss O'Murphy, mistress of Louis XV.

Antoine Watteau
THREE STUDIES OF THE HEAD OF A YOUNG GIRL WEARING A TOQUE
Red and black chalk with graphite underdrawing on the head at the left, *circa* 1716,
5½in by 8¾in (14cm by 22.3cm)
New York $852,500 (£596,154). 17.XI.86
From the collection of John R. Gaines

Thomas Rowlandson
GEORGE III AND QUEEN CHARLOTTE DRIVING THROUGH DEPTFORD
Watercolour over pen and black and grey inks and pencil on original wash line mount,
16½in by 27½in (42cm by 70cm)
London £82,500 ($143,550). 16.VII.87
From the collection of the Kimbell Art Foundation, Fort Worth, Texas

In one of his most important drawings of the 1780s, Rowlandson depicts the procession preceding George III and Queen Charlotte in the streets of Deptford. Among the crowds, the artist portrays John Jackson, the famous boxer, the Watson sisters and Jonas Hanway, who introduced the umbrella to England.

Opposite
Thomas Gainsborough, RA
STUDY OF A LADY, SEATED HOLDING A LETTER
Pencil, corners cut, 11¾in by 6⅞in (30cm by 17.5cm)
London £70,400 ($117,568). 12.III.87
From the collection of Lord Richardson, LVO

This previously unrecorded drawing is one of a group of studies drawn during the early to mid-1760s, when the artist lived in Bath.

Joseph Mallord William Turner, RA
THE LOWERZERSEE, WITH SCHWYTZ AND THE MYTHEN
Pencil and watercolour, *circa* 1843, 9in by 11¼in (22.8cm by 28.6cm)
New York $374,000 (£222,619). 21.V.87

Opposite, above
Richard Parkes Bonington
A CUTTER WITH SHIPPING IN A STIFF BREEZE OFF CALAIS
Watercolour over traces of pencil heightened with scratching out and gum arabic,
5½in by 7⅝in (14cm by 19.5cm)
London £62,700 ($104,709). 12.III.87

Below
Thomas Girtin
DURHAM CATHEDRAL
Watercolour over pencil heightened with gum arabic, *circa* 1799,
14¾in by 19½in (37.5cm by 49.5cm)
London £81,400 ($135,938). 12.III.87

John Constable, RA

EAST BERGHOLT CHURCH, SUFFOLK, WITH THE TOMB OF THE ARTIST'S PARENTS

Pencil, inscribed in another hand on an earlier mount: *East Bergholt Church. With the Tomb of Golding and Ann Constable, parents of J. Constable, by whom this was drawn Oct 28, 1818. Golding died 1816 aged 78. Ann died 1815 aged 67. By the side of their tomb are the tombs of Jas Revans, his wife, and son and daughter. Revans was Golding Constable's faithful servant,* $7\frac{7}{8}$in by $12\frac{5}{8}$in (20cm by 32cm)

London £62,700 ($99,693). 19.II.87

This is one of a group of Constable drawings, including views of Borrowdale, Stonehenge and East Bergholt, which were from the collection of the late Sir John and Lady Witt.

Opposite, above

Samuel Palmer

THE BROTHERS IN COMUS LINGERING UNDER THE VINE

Watercolour and bodycolour over pencil with gum arabic heightened with scratching out, on wove paper laid down on a wooden panel, signed, and inscribed in the artist's hand on a label attached to the backboard with a verse from *Comus* by John Milton, *circa* 1856, $20\frac{7}{8}$in by $29\frac{1}{2}$in (53cm by 75cm)

London £63,800 ($95,062). 20.XI.86

Below

John Martin, RA

THE PLAINS OF CALYPSO

Watercolour, bodycolour and gum arabic, signed and dated *1833*, $21\frac{1}{2}$in by $32\frac{1}{2}$in (54.5cm by 81.5cm)

London £90,200 ($156,948). 16.VII.87

Edward Lear
ZOGRAPHOU
Pen and brown ink and watercolour, inscribed in Greek and dated *16 × 17 Sept 1856/*
(17th Monastery), numbered in pencil *87*, and extensively inscribed with further notes,
13⅜in by 19¼in (34cm by 49cm)
London £20,900 ($34,903). 12.III.87

This is one of a group of eight watercolours of Greek monasteries from the collection of the late
Miss Margaret Crum, and were given by the artist to her ancestor, Charles Church, Dean of
Wells. The watercolours belong to a series of twenty that Lear produced during a three-week stay
on the holy island of Athos in September 1856.

Opposite
Robert Clow Todd
WOLFE'S COVE, QUEBEC, AT THE HEIGHTS OF ABRAHAM LOOKING EAST, SHOWING THE TIMBER YARD
AND THE SILLERY SHORE
Signed and dated *1840*, 29⅜in by 47½in (74.5cm by 120.5cm)
London £84,700 ($127,897). 22.X.86

Jean-Léon Pallière
A TRAIN CROSSING THE PARK, BUENOS AIRES
Watercolour over traces of pencil, signed, 12⅜in by 26⅜in (31.5cm by 67cm)
London £12,100 ($18,271). 22.X.86

Benjamin West's *Portrait of Sir Joseph Banks*

Rüdiger Joppien

Sir Joseph Banks was one of the foremost naturalists of his day. From his schooldays at Eton he had had a keen interest in botany and his personal wealth and influence enabled him to devote himself to this area of study. In 1766 he undertook an expedition to New Foundland and Labrador and, from 1768–71, accompanied Captain James Cook aboard the *Endeavour* on his first voyage around the world. When, on the eve of his departure for the South Seas, Banks was asked why he did not embark upon the Grand Tour, he is said to have replied, 'Every blockhead does that, my Grand Tour shall be one round the whole globe.'

During the voyage to Australia, the *Endeavour* made stops in Tierra del Fuego and Tahiti before proceeding to New Zealand, where the expedition stayed from 3 October 1769 to 31 March 1770. Banks found ample opportunity to collect botanical specimens and seeds as well as Maori artifacts. His journals from the voyage show him to be an accurate observer, with a profound interest in the crafts and culture of other peoples, and it is this commitment that is captured in Benjamin West's portrait, sold by Sotheby's this season (see opposite).

The full-length portrait of Banks in heroic pose was painted shortly after Banks returned to England and was exhibited at the Royal Academy in the spring of 1773 as 'A Whole length of a gentleman with a New Zealand mantle around him'. Banks is depicted surrounded by artifacts collected in the South Seas: a Tahitian chief's head-dress, a Maori paddle and a New Zealand staff on the left, and a Polynesian hatchet and a Tahitian bark-cloth beater in the foreground on the right, together with a portfolio of drawings, open to show a watercolour of a blossoming flax plant by Sydney Parkinson, the botanical draftsman who accompanied Banks on the voyage. Over his coat Banks wears a greenish striped Maori flax cloak. With his right hand, Banks points to the border, which is ornamented with a triangular *taaniko* pattern in brown, black and white, while the outer edge of the cloak is trimmed with dogs' hair. As the exhibition title of the painting confirms, besides Banks himself the cloak is the main subject of the picture.

In his journal of the voyage Banks commented on the Maori cloaks and the superior quality of the flax material, admiring both its strength and silk-like shine. He goes on to say: 'So useful a plant would doub(t)less be a great acquisition to England, especially as one might hope that it would thrive there with little trouble, as it seems hardy and affects no particular soil . . .' Other members of

Benjamin West, PRA
PORTRAIT OF SIR JOSEPH BANKS
1771, 92in by 63in (234cm by 160cm)
London £1,815,000 ($3,012,900). 11.III.87

Cook's first and indeed second voyage to the South Seas were likewise fascinated by the quality of the New Zealand flax (*Phormium tenax Forster*). In his *Voyage round the world* the young George Forster also gave a description of the Maori flax cloaks, commenting upon the black in the border pattern, obtained with a dye so durable that he felt it would be worthy of the attention of English manufacturers. South Sea artifacts were virtually unknown, since the islands had only recently been discovered, but compared with the importance attached to the flax cloak, the other ethnographical objects in the picture play a somewhat secondary role, important enough, however, for Banks to have many of them recorded in drawings by John Frederick Miller. The major part of his collection he later bequeathed to the British Museum, and outstanding objects like the Tahitian head-dress can still be seen in the Museum of Mankind in London, which also houses a cloak similar to the one in the painting, and may indeed be the cloak that belonged to Banks.

The representation of an Englishman in native dress, surrounded by exotic artifacts is relatively rare in British portraiture up to this date. Sir Joshua Reynolds and Joseph Wright of Derby painted the occasional subject in costume, and similar portraits derive from Sir Anthony van Dyck, such as *Sir Robert Shirley and Lady Theresa Shirley in Persian dress*, and *William Fielding in Hindu costume*. The exotic dress demonstrated an identification with the host country and an appreciation of the culture. There is a marked freshness of approach in the present portrait in which the subject confronts the spectator and is shown as a vigorous and progressive young man. The painting echoes the traditional formula for portraits of collectors but with a new twist, expressed in the unusual character of the objects. It thus fulfils a specific purpose, combining personal advertisement in the references to Banks' achievements as a traveller, collector and scientific naturalist, with symbolic values in which the artifacts on one side and the column and draped curtain on the other can be read as a statement on the meeting of two cultures. It is a fitting memento of Banks' own Grand Tour.

The public exhibition of the portrait was carefully staged and was timed to coincide with the issue of John Raphael Smith's mezzotint of the subject on 15 April 1773, and the publication of J. Hawkesworth's *An Account of the Voyages Undertaken by the Order of his Present Majesty for Making Discoveries in the Southern Hemisphere*, in which an account of Cook's first voyage formed the main part. The painting is the earliest known full-length representation of Banks and is remarkable in the choice of West as the artist. A young American who was enjoying considerable acclaim, West had changed the traditional concept of history painting with his *Death of General Wolfe* of 1770, in which he treated a contemporary subject in a classical manner. In 1768 he had been a founding member of the Royal Academy, and in 1772 was appointed history painter to George III. Painted at a critical time in Banks' life, the painting anticipates his importance as a leading exponent of British scientific discovery and scholarship, who was to become scientific adviser to the crown, President of the Royal Society and a founder of the Royal Horticultural Society.

Gilbert Jackson
PORTRAIT OF JOHN, BARON BELASYSE
Signed and dated *1636*, 74in by 51in (188cm by 129.5cm)
London £176,000 ($302,720). 15.VII.87
From the collection of His Grace the Duke of Hamilton and Brandon
This painting is now in the collection of the National Portrait Gallery, London.

Sir Joshua Reynolds, PRA
PORTRAIT OF WILLIAM CHARLES COLYEAR, VISCOUNT MILSINGTON (1747–1824), LATER
THIRD EARL OF PORTMORE, AS A BOY
29½in by 24⅜in (75cm by 62cm)
London £242,000 ($360,580). 19.XI.86

Opposite
George Romney
PORTRAIT OF FRANCES SAGE
1779, 58⅛in by 46⅛in (147.5cm by 117cm)
London £242,000 ($416,240). 15.VII.87

Thomas Gainsborough, RA
A WOODED LANDSCAPE WITH PEASANTS IN A COUNTRY WAGGON
1756–57, 24in by 28¾in (61cm by 73cm)
London £286,000 ($426,140). 19.XI.86

This landscape was painted as a companion to the *Wooded Landscape with Rustic Lovers*, now in the Philadelphia Museum of Art.

John Constable, RA

CLOUD STUDY

Oil on paper, inscribed and dated by the artist on the reverse: *Sept 10. 1821. Noon. Gentle wind at west/very sultry. After a heavy shower with thunder./Accumulated thunder clouds pafsing slowly away/To the south east. Very bright & hot. All the foliage/sparkling and wet.*, 10in by 12in (25.5cm by 30.5cm) London £159,500 ($237,655). 19.XI.86

Constable made a series of cloud studies at Hampstead in 1821 and 1822. Historical weather records correspond with the meticulous notes he made with reference to his studies of conditions on a particular day.

Benjamin West, PRA

ALEXANDER THE THIRD, KING OF SCOTLAND, RESCUED FROM THE FURY OF A STAG BY THE
INTREPIDITY OF COLIN FITZGERALD

Signed and dated *1786*, 145⅜in by 205½in (368.5cm by 522.5cm)

London £550,000 ($819,500). 19.XI.86

This painting is now in the collection of the National Gallery of Scotland. It was first exhibited at
the Royal Academy in 1786 having been commissioned by Francis Mackenzie, later Lord Seaforth,
in 1784 for the then considerable sum of 800 guineas. The enormous canvas depicts an anecdote
from the history of the Mackenzie clan in the thirteenth century.

George Stubbs, ARA
BARON DE ROBECK RIDING A BAY COB
Signed and dated *1791*, 40in by 50in (101.6cm by 127cm)
New York $2,420,000 (£1,484,663). 4.VI.87

Jacques-Laurent Agasse
A GREY ARAB STALLION IN AN ALPINE LANDSCAPE
29⅜in by 24⅜in (74.5cm by 62cm)
London £149,600 ($222,904). 19.XI.86

Jacques-Laurent Agasse
LORD RIVERS'S GROOM LEADING A CHESTNUT HUNTER
TOWARDS A COURSING PARTY IN HAMPSHIRE
Inscribed and dated *1808*, 26¾in by 24⅜in
(68.5cm by 62cm)
London £198,000 ($328,680). 11.III.87

Opposite
Jacques-Laurent Agasse
LORD RIVERS COURSING ON NEWMARKET HEATH
Signed with initials, 1835, 49¼in by 37in (125cm by 94cm)
New York $385,000 (£236,196). 4.VI.87

Born in Geneva, Jacques-Laurent Agasse first came to England in 1790, and settled in London
from 1800 until his death. George Pitt, 2nd Baron Rivers, was Agasse's first and most important
patron who, having encouraged Agasse to come to England, commissioned works from him
regularly after 1800. The depiction of Lord Rivers coursing on Newmarket Heath near his estates
at Stratfield Saye and Hare Park, is one of three versions that exist of the composition.

John Frederick Herring, Snr and James Pollard
THE DEAD HEAT FOR THE DONCASTER GREAT ST LEGER 1839
Oil on panel, signed and dated *1839*, and inscribed by a later hand on a label attached to the
reverse, 20½in by 29⅞in (52cm by 76cm)
London £374,000 ($643,280). 15.VII.87

The 1839 St Leger, which resulted in a dead heat between Major Yarburgh's Charles XII and
Mr Thomas Thornhill's Enclid, was one of the most celebrated races of its day. This is one of a
number of collaborations between the two artists, with Herring painting the race and Pollard the
grandstands and packed assembly of spectators beyond.

Opposite, above
John Wootton
RELEASING THE HOUNDS
17½in by 39¾in (44.5cm by 101cm)
London £99,000 ($147,510). 19.XI.86

Below
Sir Francis Grant, PRA
QUEEN VICTORIA RIDING OUT AT WINDSOR
Oil on panel, 7⅞in by 10¼in (20cm by 26cm)
London £24,750 ($36,878). 19.XI.86

This is a sketch for the large composition Grant painted for Queen Victoria in 1840, which still
hangs at Windsor Castle.

G.F. Watts' first *Hope*

Barbara Bryant

G.F. Watts' *Hope* (Fig. 1) is arguably the most famous of all Victorian paintings, yet, for most of this century, familiarity with it derived from the replica in the Tate Gallery. The unexpected rediscovery of the original version last year proved to be a landmark event in more ways than one: *Hope* not only made a record price for a work by the artist (surpassing the previous one established only a year before at Sotheby's with *Endymion*), it also achieved the highest price ever recorded for a Victorian painting. Apart from these record-breaking prices, the beauty of the painting and its unique historical importance assure its status.

In 1885, Watts described his new composition: 'I am painting a picture of Hope sitting on a globe, with bandaged eyes, playing upon a lyre which has all the strings broken but one, out of which poor little tinkle she is trying to get all the music possible, listening with all her might to the little sound. . . .' Watts did not mention the single twinkling star behind the fair-haired figure, but this detail adds another clue to the artist's intentions. The title tells us the woman represents the virtue of hope, ever optimistic in adversity. The overall blue tonality of the work has, however, often suggested a mood of sadness at variance with the title and has contributed to the misreading of the painting as 'Despair'. It is this ambiguity of expression that has always intrigued observers.

Watts completed *Hope* in 1886 when he was nearly seventy years of age. His career had already spanned five decades, beginning with portraits and history paintings in the 1830s and 1840s. Once elected a full member of the Royal Academy in 1867, Watts found increased exposure for his work and more patrons. His contemporaries always considered him a portraitist first and foremost. Watts' serious intentions in this genre can be gauged by his long-term commitment to painting at his own expense, a 'Hall of Fame' of contemporary men of achievement. He presented this great series to the National Portrait Gallery in 1895. Yet he himself held his 'symbolic' or allegorical works, such as *Love and Death*, 1877 (Whitworth Art Gallery, Manchester), in greater esteem. These works he painted for posterity. Counting *Hope* in this group, Watts wrote that it would 'form part of a series by which I endeavour to suggest and illustrate a great moral conception of human life and conditions.'

In other allegorical works, Watts relied on the interaction of figures, but from the first small pencil sketches, he was attracted by the idea of the single almost knotted figure bending over the lyre, shunning the traditional formula of symbolizing

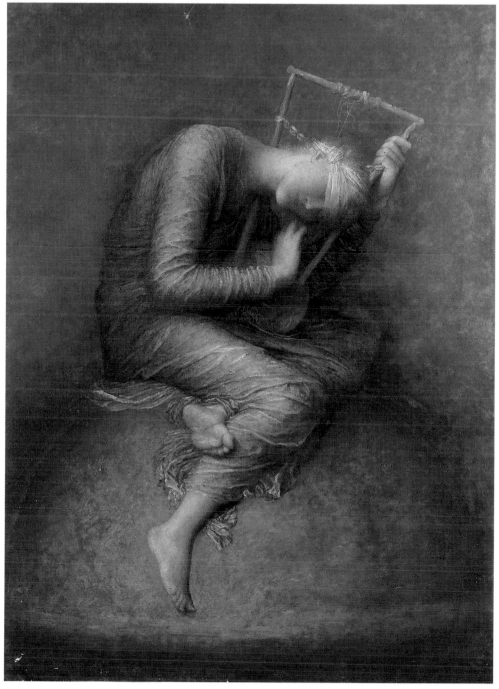

Fig. 1
George Frederic Watts, OM, RA
HOPE
1886, 59⅛in by 42⅞in (150cm by 109cm)
London £869,000 ($1,303,500). 26.XI.86

Following the sale, Sotheby's made a donation to the Watts Gallery at Compton towards the restoration of the collection.

hope with an anchor. In her biography of Watts, his wife noted that the composition had come to him more easily than almost any other. With the half-scale oil sketch (Fig. 2), the relationship of the woman, the instrument and the globe evolved, and the artist conceived the setting of blue sky and indeterminate mists. The freedom of brushwork in this preliminary work (which Watts presented to Leighton, his close friend and neighbour) made it as appealing to Watts' contemporaries, as it is to modern eyes.

Hope first appeared at the annual Grosvenor Gallery exhibition of 1886. Critics praised the extreme subtlety of the colour; in the *Academy*, Cosmo Monkhouse paid tribute to the 'tender opalescence'. F.G. Stephens in the *Athenaeum* described the effects of two light sources, with the stronger from the front balanced by the paler light of the stars: 'this exquisite illumination fuses . . . the colours, substance, and even the forms and contours of the whole, and suggests a vague dreamlike magic'. We can see what Stephens called 'tone harmony' in the original since, by a stroke of good fortune, the painting has been left untouched. Veils of gauze-like colour create depth and soften the image. The sensitive handling of the draperies is echoed by the evidence of brushstrokes in the thin paintwork of the sky and on the globe, lending a vivacity to the surface akin to that of the oil sketch.

Despite his plan to include *Hope* in his gift to the nation, Watts sold it for about £1,500 to Joseph Ruston, a member of Parliament for Lincoln, who had amassed a formidable collection of contemporary and earlier English paintings. Mrs Watts recorded that, in any case, the artist planned to paint a replica with 'certain changes'; this he did with a pupil's assistance. Watts eventually presented the later version of the painting to the Tate Gallery, along with seventeen other works, in 1897. In the replica, there are indeed minor changes. Although, at nearly six feet high, the two works are on the same scale, in the original version the figure fills more of the picture space. Watts may have reduced the figure's size in the later work to enhance her isolation. As one might expect in a replica, certain details became simplified, such as the construction of the lyre, the overall handling seems flatter and bright highlights, such as the twinkling star, have diminished.

Hope became one of Watts' most admired works. But why did the first version remain hidden for so long? After leaving the Ruston collection, the painting passed to the equally well known collector, Sir Jeremiah Colman. Only publicly exhibited once while he owned it (in Brussels in 1929), *Hope* effectively disappeared after Colman's sale in 1942. Nevertheless, the composition has had an extraordinary afterlife. Engravings and photographs of the work proved immensely popular. It even acquired inspirational connotations and was credited with curing ills and boosting downcast spirits. The image has travelled far in geographical distance: for example, a copy of the print still hangs in Teddy Roosevelt's home, Sagamore Hill in New York. Similarly, the image has travelled in time, right up to the recent past when the *Spectator*'s cartoonist cast the embattled Labour leader, Michael Foot, as Hope for the magazine's cover in October 1982. The rediscovery of the first *Hope* confirms the importance of the image, which has always survived in the popular imagination, and reveals the beauties of Watts' original treatment.

Fig. 2
George Frederic Watts, OM, RA
HOPE
Half-scale oil sketch of the composition, 26in by 21in (66cm by 53.3cm)
Reproduced courtesy of the Walker Art Gallery, Liverpool.

Ford Madox Brown
SOUTHEND (ESSEX) LOOKING TOWARDS SHEERNESS
Oil on paper, signed and inscribed *Southend;* signed, titled, dated *1858* and inscribed with the
artist's address at *13 Fortesse Road, Kentish Town, NW,* on a label on the backboard,
diameter 11⅜in (29cm)
London £126,500 ($189,750). 26.XI.86

Opposite
John William Inchbold
MID-SPRING, 'YOU SCARCE CAN SEE THE GRASS FOR FLOWERS' – TENNYSON
Oil on panel, signed; also signed and titled on a label on the backboard,
20½in by 13⅜in (52cm by 34cm)
London £24,200 ($36,300). 26.XI.86

This painting was exhibited at the Royal Academy in 1856.

Sir John Everett Millais, Bt, PRA
OPHELIA
Watercolour heightened with bodycolour, signed with monogram, 1865–66,
6⅞in by 9⅝in (17.5cm by 24.5cm)
London £74,800 ($126,412). 23.VI.87

This watercolour is a version of the oil of 1851–52, now in the Tate Gallery, London.

Opposite
John William Waterhouse, RA
GATHERING ALMOND BLOSSOM
Signed, 37⅜in by 24in (95cm by 61cm)
London £66,000 ($111,540). 23.VI.87

Albert Goodwin, RWS

BENARES

Signed, titled and dated *1899*; also signed, titled and inscribed with
the artist's address at *7 Montpelier Terrace*, on a label on the backboard,
39in by 24in (99cm by 61cm)
London £33,000 ($49,500). 26.XI.86

This painting was exhibited at the Royal Academy in 1899.

Albert Goodwin, RWS
VENICE
Mixed media on paper, laid down on panel, signed, titled and dated *1892*,
21¼in by 31⅛in (54cm by 79cm)
London £18,700 ($28,237). 16.X.86

Richard James Wyatt
A NYMPH OF DIANA TAKING A THORN OUT OF A GREYHOUND'S FOOT
Marble, signed, height 57⅛in (145cm)
London £44,000 ($74,360). 23.VI.87

This sculpture was exhibited at the Royal Academy in 1849.

Frederic, Lord Leighton, PRA, RWS
ATHLETE STRUGGLING WITH A SERPENT
Bronze, signed, inscribed and dated *1877*, height 20½in (52cm)
New York $46,750 (£29,037). 19.VI.87

This bronze group was exhibited at the Royal Academy in 1877, having first come into being in 1874 as a clay figure study for a painting.

Walter Richard Sickert, ARA
THE FAÇADE OF ST MARK'S, VENICE
Signed, *circa* 1895–96, 45½in by 60½in (115.5cm by 154cm)
London £96,800 ($170,368). 13.V.87

Opposite
Henry Herbert La Thangue, RA
PORTRAIT OF A BRETON PEASANT GIRL
Signed, *circa* 1880–81, 36in by 29⅛in (91.5cm by 74cm)
London £49,500 ($87,120). 13.V.87

Frances Hodgkins
A COUNTRY WINDOW
Signed, *circa* 1929–31, 24in by 29⅞in (61cm by 76cm)
London £68,200 ($120,032). 13.V.87

Opposite
Sir Alfred Munnings, PRA
HRH THE PRINCE OF WALES ON HORSEBACK
Signed, 1920, 50in by 42⅛in (127cm by 107cm)
London £187,000 ($282,370). 12.XI.86

Prunella Clough
FISHERMEN IN A BOAT
Signed, 1949, 55⅛in by 29⅞in
(140cm by 76cm)
London £28,600 ($50,336). 13.V.87
From the collection of
Anthony Roland

Samuel John Peploe, RSA
STILL LIFE WITH TULIPS AND ORANGES
Circa 1916, 15⅞in by 13in (40.5cm by 33cm)
Hopetoun House £35,200 ($61,600). 29.IV.87

David's *Farewell of Telemachus and Eucharis*

Robert Rosenblum

If ever an artist demonstrated the possibility of equating great art and momentous political change, it was Jacques-Louis David. In his life as in his paintings, the official propagandist for first the Revolution and then Napoleon, appeared to have been at one with the dramatic forward thrust of French history. On 12 January 1816, after the final eclipse of Napoleon, a law to banish all regicides was enacted. Fifteen days later David, one of the most famous of the regicides, went into exile in Brussels, where he was to die on 29 December 1825. There, out of touch with the political urgencies that had once fired him and his art, David, so tradition has always had it, soon lost his artistic powers.

David in exile might conceivably have created, as did his contemporary Goya under similar circumstances, an inward, resonant late style, appropriate to the great master that he was. But as the oddest irony, at least according to familiar readings of David, the history paintings of his Brussels years reverted to the erotic milieu of the rococo world he had hoped, in his revolutionary maturity, to annihilate. If it was acceptable for the generation of David's students, most notably Ingres, to explore private and sensual passions, for the master himself to take this direction could easily be interpreted as an act of self-betrayal or, at the least, as the feeble last gasp of a man who had been pushed out of the centre stage of history.

Suspicions, however, have been growing that these inherited reflexes might need to be re-examined. Was the erotic mode so exclusive to these late years? Should the conventional response of squirming with embarrassment before these ostensibly insipid late Davids not be checked more often with the reality of the paintings themselves, which, in turn, might demand to be judged by standards very unlike those established by the *Socrates* (1787) or the *Marat* (1793)? Latterly, as our own century draws closer to its ultimate decade, the assumption that only historically innovative art is worth looking at is being challenged from every side.

In the case of David, however, it was not only traditional prejudice that has kept his late works in uncomfortable oblivion, but also the fact that the visual evidence, for or against, was so spare, especially for the history paintings. To be sure, those who have been to the museums of Cleveland and Brussels and paused there before the 1817 *Cupid and Psyche* and the 1824 *Mars Disarmed by Venus and the Three Graces*, might well have had second thoughts about obliterating late David from serious

Fig. 1
Jacques-Louis David
THE FAREWELL OF TELEMACHUS AND EUCHARIS
Signed and dated *Brux 1818*, 34½in by 40in (87.6cm by 101.6cm)
New York $4,070,000 (£2,642,857). 24.II.87

This painting is now in the J. Paul Getty Museum, Malibu, California.

Fig. 2
Jacques-Louis David
CUPID AND PSYCHE
Signed and dated *Bruxelles 1817*, 72½in by 95⅛in (184.2cm by 241.6cm)
Reproduced courtesy of the Cleveland Museum of Art, Purchase, Leonard C. Hanna, Jr., Bequest

consideration: but in general, most of the later history paintings have been hidden away in private collections. Recently, though, these works have begun to surface, notably in 1981, when the Kimbell Art Museum in Forth Worth acquired the *Anger of Achilles* of 1819, a painting whose startling half-length figural composition and relentless tragic intensity immediately challenged preconceptions that in his later works David was uninventive and drawn only to boudoir narratives. And now, in the course of the past season at Sotheby's, another major history painting, the *Farewell of Telemachus and Eucharis* (Fig. 1), has turned up, presenting an opportunity for a thorough-going reappraisal of David's late work.

Painted in 1818, a year before the *Anger of Achilles*, David's *Telemachus and Eucharis* at first fits the stereotyped story of how David in Brussels turned his back upon the rigorous stoicism of his didactic painting in favour of what seemed the lesser calling of an erotic mode for private delectation. But, in fact, David had worked in this mode throughout his career. Fully defined already in 1788 in *Paris and Helen*, it survived the high-minded austerities of the revolutionary years and continued an intermittent life in such works as *Sappho and Phaon* of 1809 and the unfinished *Apelles and Campaspe* of *circa* 1813–16. Already in 1813, in Paris, David had made drawings for a painting of *Cupid and Psyche* (Fig. 2), which was only to be completed later, in Brussels, in 1817. Most of these earlier paintings were executed for aristocratic art-lovers: *Paris and Helen* for the Count d'Artois, brother of Louis XVI; *Sappho and Phaon* for the Russian Prince Youssopoff; *Cupid and Psyche* for the Italian Count Sommariva. *Telemachus and Eucharis* was also commissioned by one of this international group of connoisseurs, the Count Erwin von Schoenborn, Vice-President of the States-General of Bavaria. Unlike the earlier works, *Telemachus and Eucharis* introduces, through its use of half-length figures and its immediacy of confrontation, an almost portrait-like intimacy in which to explore face-to-face the lovers' complex feelings.

The story itself is inspired by an episode in a famous French epic, Fénelon's *Télémaque* (1699). Written as a didactic allegory to teach the author's patron, the Duke of Burgundy, the moral lessons of virtue and vice in matters of government and human relationships, this lengthy narrative recreates the adventures of the *Odyssey*. In Book 7, the hero, Ulysses' son Telemachus, finds himself shipwrecked with his wise old guide Mentor, on Calypso's island. There he meets one of Calypso's nymphs, Eucharis, and their mutual passion drives Calypso wild with jealousy. Mentor persuades Telemachus that it is his higher duty to escape from the island and from Calypso, to continue his search for his father. From these picaresque adventures, David has imagined the seclusion of Telemachus and Eucharis in a grotto during a hunt, where they savour their reciprocal lust. Both physically and psychologically Telemachus struggles, tilting towards Eucharis and grasping her thigh, but also looking dreamily towards the spectator in what we know must be his resolution to leave. Eucharis is far more distressed, clasping her arms about his neck and closing her eyes against his shoulder in a final swoon of possessive love.

For post-Freudian and probably pre-Freudian eyes, the picture is fraught with sexual innuendo, not only in the intricate half-embrace and the revealing slits from waist to thigh in Eucharis's dishevelled tunic, but in the prominent attributes of the hunt: the upright spear and the quiver on which David has signed his name, and the curve of the hunting horn on which he has inscribed *Brux 1818*. *Cupid and Psyche* had already detailed such a complex amorous disentanglement; but what is new here is the directness of the spectator's involvement. Moving from full-length to half-length figures and compressing the couple forward against the narrow grotto background, David forces us to be confidants to this scene. The distancing proscenium and perspective recessions of his earlier staged spectacles have been left behind, and we are confronted by the intimacy of exposed flesh and feeling.

Although the subject is nominally an erotic one, it nevertheless conveys the sense of moral polarities familiar in David's earlier masterpieces, especially that between masculine rectitude and feminine weakness. Telemachus, like Hercules, must wrestle between the paths of virtue and vice; and if the higher-minded choice is inevitable, it is not easy. Visually speaking, the strong rhymes and contrasts of David's pictorial genius are no less apparent, whether in the duality of red tunic and blue toga, blond and brunet hair, frontal and profile views, or in the interlocking of emphatic, criss-crossing axes that almost in themselves tell the story of joining and separating magnetisms. Even the elegant white hunting dog's head falls into axial as well as emotional place, pointing upwards in tandem with the diagonal that brings the would-be lovers' heads together, while casting a baleful glance at them. As for the conflicting dualities that so often animate David's art, *Telemachus and Eucharis* offers a familiar contrast of abstract and empirical extremes. If Eucharis's facial type clings to an imagined classical ideal, Telemachus's soft and fleshy features bear the marks of a specific teenage model. And if the treatment of anatomy seems as polished and perfected as in a classical marble, the details of hair, drapery and the accessories of the hunt have the material, palpable quality of theatrical props, turning the picture into a kind of *tableau vivant*. As is often the case with David, the ghost of Caravaggio is resurrected in the fusion of an underlying sense of geometric order and an insistence on recording sharp-focus visual truths.

It is obvious that David was fascinated by this half-length format for classical history painting, for he essayed it the following year in the *Anger of Achilles*, a tragic quartet of half-length figures whose insistent proximity obliges us to examine the wide spectrum of emotions depicted in this drama of family conflict. But the originality of *Telemachus and Eucharis* had issue not only in David's own work, but in that of his devoted pupil, Antoine-Jean Gros, who in 1816 was left with the heavy task of maintaining his master's Paris studio. Gros, too, was commissioned by the same Bavarian patron, the Count von Schoenborn, for whom David had painted *Telemachus and Eucharis*. In 1821 Gros completed what is virtually a thematic and compositional pendant to David's *Telemachus and Eucharis*, a *Bacchus and Ariadne* (Fig. 3). Even the dimensions of Gros' painting correspond closely to David's. It is ironic to note that in 1822, both David and Gros made replicas of these paintings, an indication of their popularity.

Despite its private destination, *Telemachus and Eucharis* was immediately exhibited publicly in 1818 at charity benefits in Ghent and Brussels. After David's death, either the original or the second version was shown in Paris in 1826 at another benefit, for the cause of Greek independence, in the illustrious company of Delacroix's *Greece on the Ruins of Missolonghi*. In 1846, it was again shown in Paris with a group of modern French painters at the Musée Classique du Bazar Bonne-Nouvelle, this time to benefit needy artists. It was none other than Baudelaire who, in his review of the show, claimed that *Telemachus and Eucharis*, along with the *Socrates*, the *Marat*, and the *Napoleon at St Bernard*, were the four most important paintings by David of the ten on view. He also referred to it as a charming picture, which seemed to want to rival the delicate, dreamlike paintings of Guérin, a painter of Gros' generation who, like many others, translated the premises of Davidian style into a vehicle for

Fig. 3
Antoine-Jean Gros
BACCHUS AND ARIADNE
Signed and dated *1820*, 33½in by 39⅜in (85cm by 100cm)
Reproduced courtesy of Phoenix Art Museum; Museum purchase with funds provided by an
anonymous donor

mythological fantasies. But what is no less remarkable than David seemingly
following the erotic path adopted by the generation he had spawned, was the
emphatic physical and psychological closeness of his classical lovers, who are only
a glance and a touch away from the spectator. To be sure, looking backwards to
David's own past, *Telemachus and Eucharis* may be viewed as a last, moribund stage
in the eclipse of the master's idealism, but facing the future of French painting, it is
more wisely viewed as a major step towards a vigorous new realism that, by mid-
century, would triumph with Courbet.

Horace Vernet
THE START OF THE RACE OF THE RIDERLESS HORSES *or* LA MOSSA
1820, 29¼in by 39in (74.3cm by 99cm)
New York $484,000 (£314,286). 24.II.87

Jean-Léon Gérôme
SUMMER AFTERNOON ON THE LAKE
Signed, *circa* 1895, 23½in by 36¼in (59.7cm by 92.1cm)
New York $374,000 (£242,857). 24.II.87

Jean-Baptiste-Camille Corot
SMYRNE-BOURNABAT
Signed, 1873, $31\frac{7}{8}$in by $43\frac{1}{4}$in (81cm by 110cm)
London £825,000 ($1,394,250). 30.VI.87

Gustave Courbet
LA VAGUE, MER HOULEUSE AU CRÉPUSCULE
Signed, 1869, 29¼in by 35¾in (74.3cm by 90.8cm)
New York $440,000 (£261,905). 21.V.87

Jean-François Millet
PETITE BERGERE TRICOTANT
Pastel on paper, stamped with initials, *circa* 1872–74, 13in by 10in (33cm by 25.4cm)
New York $286,000 (£201,408). 28.X.86

Jean-Baptiste-Camille Corot
VILLE D'AVRAY – LE BATEAU QUITTANT LA RIVE
Signed, *circa* 1865–70, 23½in by 39in (59.7cm by 99cm)
New York $605,000 (£360,119). 21.V.87
From the collection of the Kimbell Art Foundation, Fort Worth, Texas

Ferdinand Hodler
DER REDNER (THE ORATOR)
Signed, 1913, 49¼in by 29¾in (125cm by 75.5cm)
Zurich SF253,000 (£105,417: $147,953). 27.XI.86

Christen Købke
PORTRAIT OF DR JOHANN HENNING KJETHIL HJARDEMAAL
Signed and dated *1833*, 13¼in by 10in (33.5cm by 25.5cm)
London £50,600 ($75,900). 26.XI.86

Albert Edelfelt
UNDER THE BIRCHES
Signed and dated *PARIS 1882*, 23¼in by 32⅛in (59cm by 81.5cm)
London £385,000 ($646,800). 25.III.87

Anders Zorn
PORTRAIT OF ELIZABETH SHERMAN CAMERON
Signed and dated *1900*, 57½in by 45¼in (146cm by 115cm)
New York $286,000 (£170,238). 21.V.87
From the collection of the National Museum of American Art, Smithsonian Institution

Carl Larsson

MIDVINTERBLOT

Oil on two canvases, 1911–15, overall size 254¼in by 537in (640cm by 1360cm)
London £880,000 ($1,478,400). 25.III.87

Commissioned in 1893 for the National Museum in Stockholm, this painting marks the climax of
Larsson's career. The subject was intended as an allegory of winter, based on Swedish mythology,
and depicts the legendary King Domalde offering himself as a sacrifice to the gods to save his
people from famine. However, the composition excited great controversy and, rather than
compromise, Larsson refused to complete the decorations for the National Museum. With the
passage of time *Midvinterblot* can now be recognized as one of the most important expressions of
Scandinavian nationalism, as well as being a major work in the wider European tradition of
Symbolism and Art Nouveau.

Wilhelm List
NIGHT RISES FROM THE SEA
Tempera and silver paint on canvas, signed,
circa 1904, 62¼in by 25⅜in (158cm by 64.5cm)
London £88,000 ($132,000). 8.X.86

Claude Monet
MOULIN A VENT ET BATEAUX A ZAANDAM
Signed and dated *72*, 18⅛in by 29in (46cm by 73.7cm)
London £1,155,000 ($1,674,750). 2.XII.86

Although dated 1872, Monet painted this picture in 1871, during his first trip to Holland.
The painting is now in the collection of the Ny Carlsberg Glyptotek, Copenhagen.

Camille Pissarro
JARDINS POTAGERS A L'HERMITAGE, PONTOISE
Signed and dated *1873*, 21¼in by 28¾in (54cm by 73cm)
London £770,000 ($1,262,800). 30.VI.87

Pierre-Auguste Renoir
PLACE DE LA TRINITE
Signed, 1875, 20¼in by 24¾in (51.5cm by 62.8cm)
London £1,870,000 ($2,711,500). 2.XII.86

This is one of several views of the streets of Paris painted by Renoir during his great period of
Impressionism in the 1870s.

Opposite
Pierre-Auguste Renoir
LA COIFFURE
Signed, 1888, 31⅞in by 22¾in (81cm by 57.8cm)
New York $3,520,000 (£2,461,538). 18.XI.86

Henri Le Sidaner
LA SERENADE, VENISE
Signed, 1905, 53⅞in by 72⅜in (137cm by 184cm)
London £247,500 ($400,900). 1.VII.87

Opposite
Claude Monet
LE PALAIS DARIO, VENISE
Signed and dated *1908*, 31⅞in by 26in (81cm by 66cm)
London £1,760,000 ($2,552,000). 2.XII.86

Paul Gauguin
LE JARDIN EN HIVER, RUE CARCEL
Signed and dated *83*, 46in by 35½in (116.9cm by 90cm)
New York $2,090,000 (£1,259,036). 11.V.87

Paul Cézanne
CARRIERE DE BIBEMUS
Circa 1898–1900, 25⅝in by 21¼in (65cm by 54cm)
New York $3,290,000 (£1,981,928). 11.V.87
From the collection of the late Sam Spiegel

Gustav Klimt
BILDNIS VON ROSE VON
ROSTHORN–FRIEDMANN
Circa 1900–1901,
55⅛in by 31½in (140cm by 80cm)
London £1,760,000 ($2,956,800).
31.III.87

Opposite
Egon Schiele
PORTRÄT DES MALERS ANTON PESCHKA
Oil, silver and gold-bronze paint on
canvas, signed and dated *1909*,
43¼in by 39⅜in (110cm by 100cm)
London £1,760,000 ($2,956,800).
31.III.87

Gustav Klimt
SCHLOSS KAMMER AM ATTERSEE II
Signed, *circa* 1909, 43¼in by 43¼in (110cm by 110cm)
London £3,300,000 ($5,412,000). 30.VI.87

Opposite
Gustav Klimt
BILDNIS EUGENIA (MÄDA) PRIMAVESI
Signed, 1912, 55in by 33⅜in (139.7cm by 86cm)
New York $3,850,000 (£2,319,277). 11.V.87

Henri Matisse
LA DANSE
Découpage with indian ink, watercolour and gouache, signed, 1939,
19¼in by 24¼in (49cm by 61.6cm)
New York $935,000 (£653,846). 17.XI.86
From the collection of John R. Gaines

This is a small cut-out replica of Matisse's large painting *La Danse*, 1910, now in
the Hermitage, Leningrad.

Opposite
Pablo Picasso
LA MATERNITE
Signed, 1921, 40¼in by 33⅞in (102.1cm by 86cm)
New York $3,520,000 (£2,120,482). 11.V.87

Kees van Dongen
UN BAL DES 'ANNEES FOLLES'
Signed, *circa* 1913–14, 57½in by 40⅞in (146cm by 103.8cm)
New York $990,000 (£692,308). 18.XI.86

Marc Chagall
PAYSAGE DE PARIS
Signed and dated *1978;* also signed on the reverse, 51¼in by 63¾in (130.2cm by 162cm)
New York $1,430,000 (£861,446). 11.V.87

Emil Nolde
BLUMENGARTEN, FRAU IN ROT-VIOLETTEM KLEID
Signed and titled on the stretcher, 1908, 22½in by 33¼in (57cm by 84.5cm)
London £517,000 ($847,880). 30.VI.87

Emil Nolde
MEER MIT ABENDHIMMEL UND SEGELBOOT
Watercolour on Japan paper, signed, *circa* 1930, 13¼in by 17⅞in (33.7cm by 45.5cm)
New York $165,000 (£116,197). 19.XI.86
From the collection of Charles Tabachnick

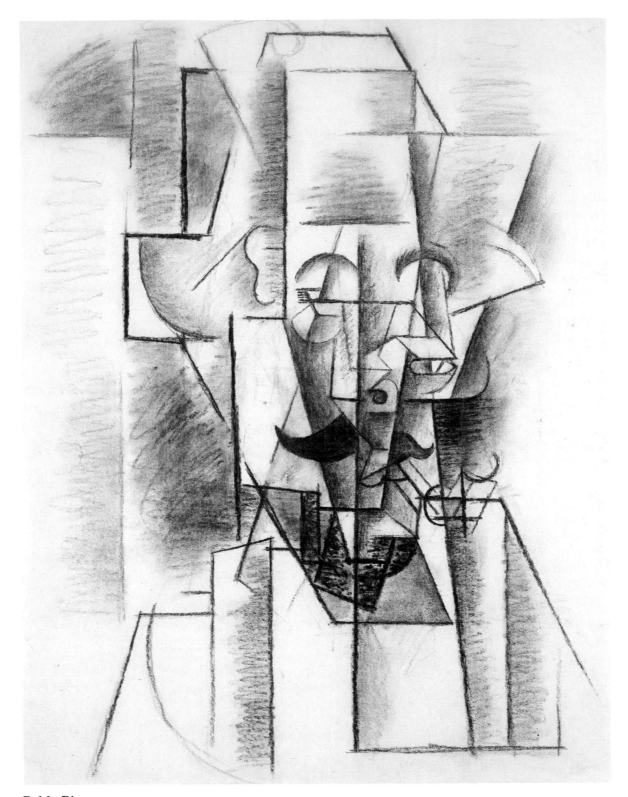

Pablo Picasso
TETE D'HOMME A LA PIPE
Charcoal, signed on the reverse, 1912, 24¾in by 18¾in (62cm by 47.6cm)
New York $1,650,000 (£1,153,846). 17.XI.86
From the collection of John R. Gaines

Georges Braque
FEMME LISANT
Signed on the
reverse, 1911,
51⅛in by 31⅞in
(130cm by 81cm)
London
£6,600,000
($9,570,000).
2.XII.86

The Studio of René Magritte

Julian Barran

In a modest suburban villa, René Magritte lived from 1951 until his death in 1967. He was survived by his widow, Georgette Berger, who remained in residence in the 'Magritte shrine' until her death in February 1986. The only hint of the unusual around the exterior of the house was a tree stump whose girth seemed to be out of proportion with the garden path beside which it was set. The observant visitor would notice, however, that next to it lay an axe; or rather a root of the stump trapped the axe's shaft beneath it. At this point he would realize that he was entering '*La Domaine d'Arnheim*', the fantastic world of René Magritte, for the axe and the tree stump were made of bronze (Fig. 1).

This sculpture was one of the 276 lots from the collection of the remaining contents of the Belgian surrealist's studio, sold for a total of £2,318,800 ($3,802,832). Magritte was a horder, surrounding himself with those inspirational pointers which peopled his own personal world of '*l'art fantastique*'. In addition to a mass of memorabilia, the sale included oil paintings, works in gouache and watercolour and on paper. *Les Travaux d'Alexandre* was one of four bronzes among a quantity of other material, including Magritte's bowler hat, the artist's easel, paintbrushes and unused canvases. Interspersed throughout the sale were pencil studies for his major compositions, providing a unique study opportunity for scholars and students.

The development of Magritte as an intellectual and as a painter was closely charted by this sale. His involvement with the Cubo–Futurist movement at the start of his career, was recorded by *La Femme ayant une rose à la place du coeur*, an oil of 1924, and two works in coloured crayon of approximately the same date, *Femme assise* and *Femme debout*. These were followed by examples of his pure surrealist works, among them, untitled, a heavy, dark painting inscribed with the words, *La Pipe*. This harsh, almost monochrome painting is one of Magritte's first '*jeux de mot*'. The artist's work from the '30s was represented by *Objet peint-oeil*, in which the deftness of his intellect is matched by his artistic brilliance. His later periods are represented by *Jean-Marie* of the '*époque vache*' and *Le prêtre marié*.

The manuscript section of the sale included both letters from the artist's contemporaries and others from him to his wife, an important series dating from before and just after they got married. There were also exhibition catalogues, magazines and endless reviews, an ostrich egg, toy railway trains, hand-painted chairs, painted bottles (Fig. 2) and even an unworn stetson hat. But as the auctioneer's gavel fell on the last lot, Magritte's secret still seemed totally illusive.

Fig. 1
René Magritte
LES TRAVAUX D'ALEXANDRE
Bronze, signed and dated *1967*, stamped *E. A.* and inscribed *Galerie Iolas*, height $23\frac{5}{8}$in (60cm)
London £72,600 ($124,146). 2.VII.87

Left to right
René Magritte
OBJET PEINT: BOUTEILLE
Oil on glass, *circa* 1950–60, height 11⅞in (30cm), £39,600 ($67,716)
OBJET PEINT: BOUTEILLE
Oil on glass, *circa* 1945, height 11½in (29cm), £52,800 ($90,288)
OBJET PEINT: BOUTEILLE
Oil on glass, *circa* 1941, height 11½in (29cm), £112,200 ($191,862)

The painted bottles from the studio of René Magritte were sold in London on 2 July 1987.

René Magritte
LA CLAIRVOYANCE
Signed, 21¼in by 25⅝in (54cm by 65cm)
London £418,000 ($685,520). 30.VI.87

La Clairvoyance, a true self portrait, was painted at some time between May and October 1936.

Paul Klee
FREUNDLICHER ORT
Gouache and watercolour on chalk-primed paper, mounted on paper, mounted on board, signed, dated and numbered *1919.1*, sheet size 7⅝in by 9¼in (19.4cm by 23.5cm)
New York $330,000 (£197,605). 12.V.87

Wassily Kandinsky
COMPOSITION
Watercolour and indian ink, signed with initials, *circa* 1915–17, 9in by 13⅜in (22.8cm by 34cm)
London £214,500 ($311,025). 3.XII.86

Piet Mondrian
COMPOSITION IN A SQUARE WITH RED CORNER. PICTURE NO. 3, 1938
Signed with initials and dated *38;* also inscribed on the stretcher by the artist *Picture N: III Piet Mondrian 38,* diagonal 58⅜in (148.3cm)
New York $5,060,000 (£3,538,462). 18.XI.86
From the collection of the late James Johnson Sweeney

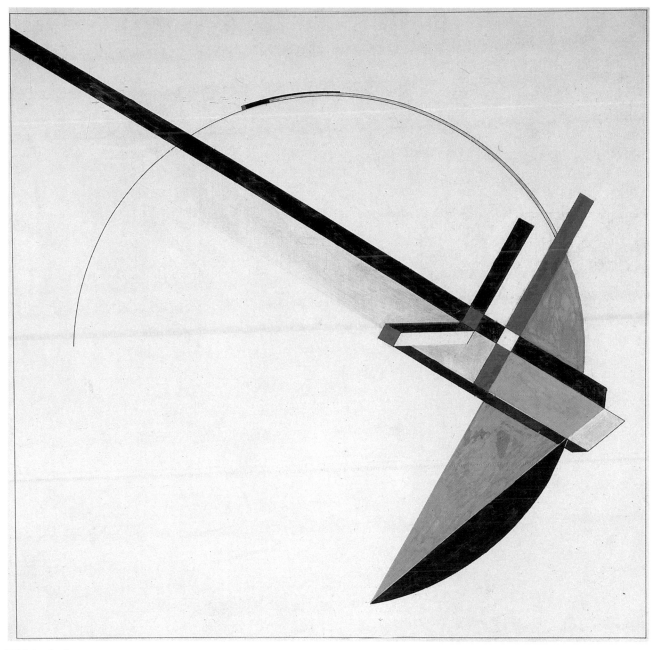

El Lissitzky
COMPOSITION
Gouache and pen and ink and pencil, *circa* 1924, 17⅞in by 17⅞in (45.5cm by 45.5cm)
London £134,200 ($222,772). 2.IV.87

Joan Miró
FEMME DANS LA NUIT
Signed, titled and dated *18-4-45* on the reverse, 51¼in by 76⅜in (130.2cm by 194cm)
New York $2,530,000 (£1,769,231). 18.XI.86
From the collection of the late James Johnson Sweeney

This is one of a series of nineteen paintings generally referred to by the same title, *Woman in the Night*.
They were all painted between January and October 1945.

Opposite
Joan Miró
FEMME
Oil, tempera, pastel and pencil on heavy paper, signed; also signed, titled and dated *4/IX/73*
on the reverse, 39⅜in by 25⅝in (100cm by 65cm)
Madrid Pta27,440,000 (£142,044: $202,107). 9.XII.86
This painting, from the collection of Pilar Miró, was sold in aid of the Pilar and Joan Miró Foundation,
Palma, Mallorca.

Henry Moore: 1898–1986

Ann Garrould

In 1972 a journalist asked Henry Moore what he thought about the enormous prices then being paid for his work. Moore replied, 'It astonishes me . . . It's a slight embarrassment and I wish it hadn't come to this because it makes one conscious of prices and I don't want to be. I'm interested, of course – you can't not be. But, you know, some of these sculptures I sold originally for next to nothing. Late in Degas' life, paintings he'd practically given away began to fetch world record prices. After one such sale, someone asked him how he felt – "I feel like the horse that's won the Derby and been given a lump of sugar".'

Prices paid for Moore's work continued to rise during the following decade. In 1983, the year in which Moore's eighty-fifth birthday was celebrated with a major retrospective exhibition in the Metropolitan Museum of Art in New York, one of his sculptures was sold for a world record price for work by a living sculptor. An interviewer telephoned from New York: 'Mr Moore, how do you feel about your sculpture fetching a world record price?' 'Well I'm glad it's a world record high and not a world record low,' Moore replied, laughing; then he turned to pick up the drawing on which he had been working. Underlying his amazement at the increasingly high prices his work fetched, one sensed a gentle glow of satisfaction; he too had won the Derby and been rewarded with his lump of sugar.

Moore's working life spanned more than sixty years. During this period three major themes preoccupied him; the reclining figure, the mother and child and the internal/external form. Moore used to say that the reclining figure gave a sculptor far more freedom to experiment with form than did a standing figure, anchored to the ground by its feet, or a seated figure, which required some credible support, however simple its form. Of the mother and child theme Moore would say that some of the earliest known sculptures depict the relationship which celebrates the continuing of the human race. The third theme required more explanation. Moore talked of the petals of a flower surrounding the delicate pistil and stamen, and also of visits to the Wallace Collection in London to look at the suits of armour and to reflect on how the hard carapace of metal protected the vulnerable body of its wearer. Essentially this theme was concerned with a larger form which protected or enclosed a smaller one. The link with the mother and child theme was obvious.

Fig. 1
Henry Moore, OM, CH
RECLINING FIGURE (FESTIVAL)
Bronze, 1951, length 93¼in (237cm)
New York $1,760,000 (£1,230,769). 18.XI.86

This figure was commissioned by the Arts Council of Great Britain for the 1951 Festival of Britain and cast in an edition of five. It is one of a comparatively small number of works that Moore looked upon as keys to a particular period.

Moore delighted in exploring the possibilities offered by these themes. The nine reclining figures in the two auctions that took place at Sotheby's in London and New York at the end of 1986 show him manipulating the human form, portraying it in repose, or watchful and alert, or falling wounded and dying. The earliest *Reclining Figure* sold, cast originally in 1939, looks back to one of the first influences on Moore, that of Pre-Columbian art. He never forgot the impression made on him by the sculpture of the Mexican deity, Chac Mool, who lies supported on elbows, buttocks and feet, gazing impassively at the spectator. From September 1939 until the end of the second world war, Moore produced very little sculpture. When, after the war, he was again able to obtain bronze for casting, it is interesting to note that he returned to the subject of the reclining figure. In this particular post-war figure,

Fig. 2
Henry Moore, OM, CH
THE FALLING WARRIOR
Bronze on a wood base covered in copper sheeting, 1956–57, length 60⅜in (153.5cm)
London £385,000 ($558,250). 2.XII.86
From the collection of Maurice and Ann Cooke

the upper part of the body is twisted to face the spectator, giving a sense of tension to the sculpture. The breasts are holes, leading the eye through the figure and making the spectator conscious of its three-dimensionality. In the following five or six years Moore moved towards producing sculptures in which form and space were, as he put it, 'completely dependent on and inseparable from each other.' Where the holes in earlier works had been features in themselves, by the time he produced the *Reclining Figure (Festival)* (Fig. 1) in 1951 'space and form are so naturally fused that they are one.'

Fig. 3
Henry Moore, OM, CH
HELMET HEAD NO. 2
Bronze, 1955, height 13¼in (33.7cm)
London £170,500 ($247,225). 2. XII.86
From the collection of Maurice and Ann Cooke

Moore realized that by dividing the human form into two or three or even four parts, he could obtain many more three-dimensional variations than were possible with the single unified figure. The spaces between the component parts of the body became as important as the holes in his earlier sculptures: they had new dynamic vitality. So, too, the position of the shield by the head of the *Falling Warrior* (Fig. 2) adds to the dramatic quality of the sculpture, as support for the still-living body.

In the years preceding the second world war Moore had used drawings as the starting point for his sculptures. During the war he had begun to model in terracotta choosing to work on a scale that he could hold comfortably in his hand, say eight to ten inches long or high, working on the sculpture in the round, creating the form in three dimensions. This method of working obviated one of the difficulties he encountered when he drew his ideas for sculpture. In later years he commented that the first view of a sculpture he recorded on paper became in his mind the dominant view. He then had to think very hard about how the sculpture would look from behind, from each end, from on top and from below.

Modelling in terracotta or plaster eliminated this problem since all aspects developed simultaneously. Moore always insisted that, in his own mind, there was never any change of scale between the plaster maquette and the over-life-size bronze. For him, the maquette he held in his hand *was* the over-life-size sculpture. Quite simply, he would say, it was more convenient to make alterations to an eight-inch plaster maquette than to have to walk round an eight-foot long armature, adding or subtracting plaster to create the desired form. However, as the sculpture grew in size, Moore did make certain modifications. The human eye and intellect can comprehend one view of a small maquette in its totality; once that maquette is enlarged four or five times, the eye comprehends only one section of the sculpture at a time, since the other sections are inevitably out of focus. By the time the maquette has become an eight-foot long (or high) sculpture the relationship between sculpture and spectator is totally altered. Moore had learnt this as a student when he visited Pisa in 1925 and saw the great sculptures of Giovanni Pisano set sixty feet above the ground around the Baptistery in the Campo dei Miracoli. It was a lesson he was never to forget. From Pisano, too, he learnt that the figures he carved would have to be capable of holding their poses for eternity. In Moore's great works one finds the same qualities of humanity, timelessness and universality that he had seen in the Baptistery sculptures.

Two of the sculptures sold at Sotheby's stand outside the reclining figure category. The *Helmet Head No.2* (Fig.3) represents the internal/external theme in Moore's oeuvre. The outer form can be seen either as a helmet or indeed as a bony skull. The deep shadow inside the concave form endows the sculpture with a tremendous sense of mystery and foreboding. The *Knife-Edge Two-Piece* (Fig. 4) is one of Moore's less obviously representational sculptures. Moore himself disliked hearing some of his works described as 'abstract'. He would say that *all* art is to some extent abstract and preferred to avoid the word in connection with his own sculpture. Here the knife-edge form clearly owes much of its inspiration to some of the *objets trouvés* in

Fig. 4
Henry Moore, OM, CH
KNIFE-EDGE TWO-PIECE
Bronze, signed and numbered *2/10* on the base, 1962, length 28⅛in (71.5cm)
London £137,500 ($199,375). 2.XII.86
From the collection of Maurice and Ann Cooke

This is a working model for the larger version of the sculpture completed in 1965.

knife-edge form clearly owes much of its inspiration to some of the *objets trouvés* in Moore's studios, in particular perhaps to a bird's breastbone which lies on a studio shelf amongst a motley collection of shells, pebbles, flints and other bones.

Moore often used to say that all art should have a certain mystery, that it should not be too accessible to a perfunctory glance, that it should demand an effort on the part of the spectator. He would nonetheless have been surprised, and perhaps pleased, to learn that it was the two less representational works that sold for sums considerably above the estimated prices.

Jacques Lipchitz
FIGURE
Bronze, signed, numbered *0/0* and
stamped with the foundry mark
Modern Art Foundry, New York N.Y.,
height 83⅞in (213cm)
New York $1,100,000 (£769,231).
18.XI.86
From the collection of Mr and Mrs
Irving C. Deal

Begun in 1926, *Figure* is a development
of Lipchitz's *Ploumanach* of 1926, and
summarizes many of the artist's ideas
dating back to 1915.

Opposite
Arshile Gorky
PORTRAIT OF Y.D.
Signed and dated *45*, 32in by 25in
(81.3cm by 63.5cm)
New York $572,000 (£340,476). 4.V.87

Jackson Pollock
NUMBER 26, 1950
Oil on masonite, signed and dated *50*, 34½in by 26½in (87.6cm by 67.3cm)
New York $2,750,000 (£1,636,905). 4.V.87
From the Playboy Enterprises Corporate Collection

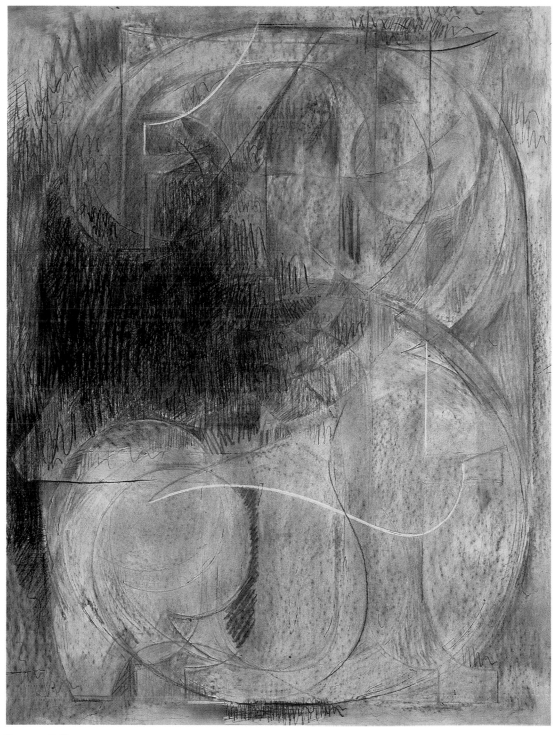

Jasper Johns
0 THROUGH 9
Charcoal and pastel on paper, 1961, 54⅛in by 41⅝in (137.5cm by 105.7cm)
New York $880,000 (£611,111). 11.XI.86
From the collection of the late Robert C. Scull

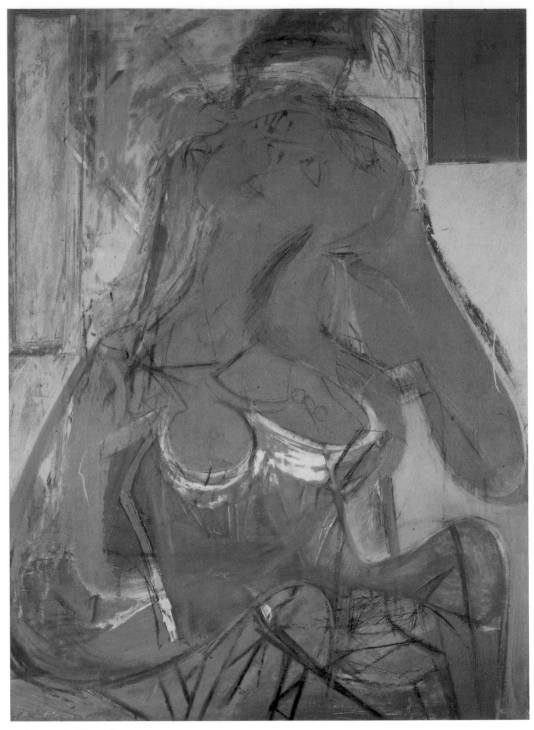

Willem de Kooning
PINK LADY
Oil and charcoal on panel, signed, *circa* 1944, 48¼in by 35¼in (122.5cm by 89.5cm)
New York $3,630,000 (£2,160,714). 4.V.87
From the collection of Betty Warner and Stanley K. Sheinbaum, Trustees

Jean Dubuffet
IL FLUTE SUR LA BOSSE
Oil on masonite, 45⅝in by 35in (116cm by 89cm)
London £319,000 ($478,500). 4.XII.86

Constant
UNTITLED
Signed, *circa* 1949, 33½in by 27¾in (85cm by 70.5cm)
London £187,000 ($306,680). 2.VII.87

Asger Jorn
ALLEGRETTO FURBO
Signed and dated *64*, 63¾in by 51⅛in (162cm by 130cm)
London £170,500 ($255,750). 4.XII.86

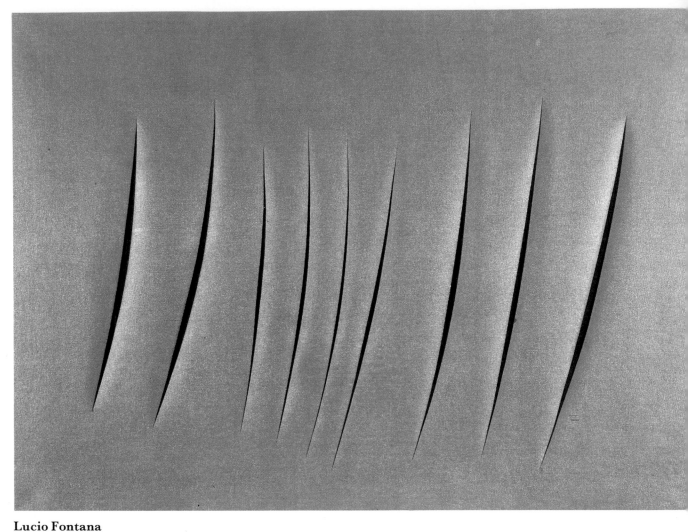

Lucio Fontana
CONCETTO SPAZIALE
Signed, titled and inscribed *ATTESE 1 + 1 S4 ATU* on the reverse, 1962,
38¼in by 51¼in (97cm by 130cm)
London £154,000 ($252,560). 2.VII.87

Opposite
Yves Klein
IKB 74
Blue pigment in synthetic resin on fabric laid down on panel, signed, titled, inscribed *monochrome*
and dated *1958* on the reverse, 78¾in by 55⅛in (200cm by 140cm)
London £638,000 ($1,046,320). 2.VII.87

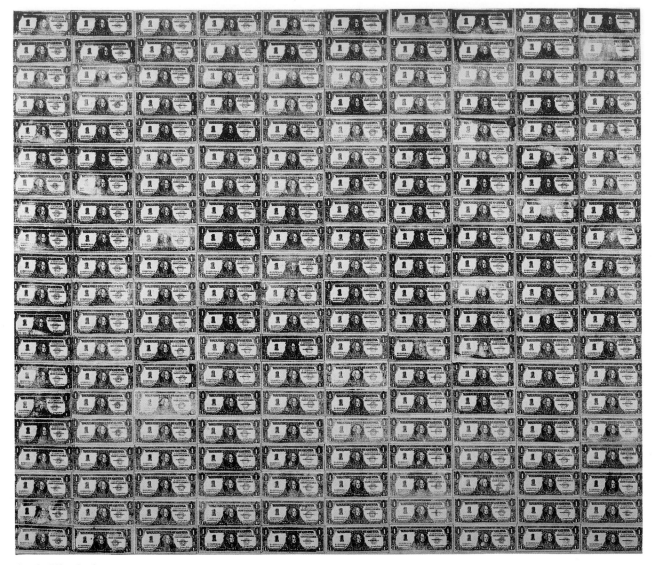

Andy Warhol
200 ONE DOLLAR BILLS
Synthetic polymer silkscreened on canvas, 1962, 80¼in by 92¼in (204cm by 234.5cm)
New York $385,000 (£267,361). 11.XI.86
From the collection of the late Robert C. Scull

Opposite
Jasper Johns
DOUBLE FLAG
1962, 98¼in by 72¼in (249.7cm by 183.7cm)
New York $1,760,000 (£1,222,222). 11.XI.86
From the collection of the late Robert C. Scull

The Scull Collections of Contemporary art

Lucy Mitchell-Innes

As collectors, Mrs Ethel Redner Scull and the late Robert C. Scull have had a remarkable influence, both on the success of the Pop and Minimalist movements and on the development of the international auction market for contemporary art. Of the three sales of property from the Scull collections that have been held at Sotheby's since 1965, the 1973 auction and those of the past season will long be remembered for their impact on the contemporary market.

In October 1973, Robert Scull consigned fifty major works by contemporary artists, many of whom had never appeared before at public auction. At that time, auction galleries were virtually untried as a market-place for the resale of contemporary art, which principally changed hands privately. Surrounded by scepticism and controversy, the sale received unprecedented attention in the art world and in the international press. An astonishing total of $2,250,000 was achieved, with works by Jasper Johns, Andy Warhol and Robert Rauchenberg bringing world record prices. Johns's *Double White Map* fetched $250,000, the highest price of the sale, which remained a record for the artist until November 1985 when *Painting with Ruler and Grey* brought $687,000. In fact, the high expectations for Johns's work set by the 1973 sale led to a number of paintings of lesser quality failing to sell in the intervening years. The record $125,000 paid for the Warhol *Flower* was not surpassed for a decade.

The November 1986, Scull sales had a similar impact, revitalizing the contemporary auction market and achieving unexpected success for works by artists whose results at auction previously had been unpredictable. The two-day sale began with ten works, the property of Mrs Ethel Redner Scull, among them five by Jasper Johns, including a black and white *Target*, a gift to the Sculls from the artist, and a drawing for the famous painting *False Start* that they had once owned. *False Start* illustrates the way the artist arrives at a title for his paintings. The term comes from a racing print that hung in the Cedar Bar, a popular haunt for artists in the 1950s and '60s. The title may also refer ironically to the stylistic changes that appeared for the first time in *False Start* and its companion painting *Jubilee*, which moved away from the imagery of flags, targets and numbers of the preceding years. Both were painted in 1959, the year after Johns's enormously successful show at Castelli, where Alfred Barr purchased several paintings for the Museum of Modern Art.

The high point of the November auctions was unquestionably the sale of Johns's *Out the Window* (Fig. 1). Like *False Start* and *Jubilee*, *Out the Window* dates from

Fig. 1
Jasper Johns
OUT THE WINDOW
Encaustic and newspaper collage on canvas, 1959, 54½in by 40⅛in (138.5cm by 102cm)
New York $3,630,000 (£2,520,833). 10.XI.86
From the collection of Ethel Redner Scull

This painting realized a record price for a work by a living artist and for a post-war contemporary painting.

Fig. 2
Bruce Nauman
UNTITLED
Beeswax over plaster with rope, 1967, overall size 16in by 19in by 6in (40.7cm by 48.3cm by 15.2cm)
New York $220,000 (£152,778). 10.XI.86
From the collection of Ethel Redner Scull

Fig. 3
James Rosenquist
F-111
Oil on canvas with aluminium, 1964–65, 10ft by 86ft (304.8cm by 2621.3cm)
New York $2,090,000 (£1,451,389). 11.XI.86
From the collection of the late Robert C. Scull

1959 and manifests Johns's new painterly style and abstract use of colour, a significant change from the tighter surfaces and specific use of colour in his earlier work. Johns executed *Out the Window* in encaustic, a combination of hot wax and pigment, which was his preferred medium. In contrast to oil, used for *False Start* and *Jubilee*, encaustic dries very quickly, allowing discreet layers of paint to be built up without smearing. In this work, the artist also first introduced the three-panel format a compositional device of which Johns has said, 'The conservative treatment is partly to do with the idea of play, showing a thing in different ways, and partly to do with my lack of invention.' The new direction that characterized the paintings of 1959 was duly noted by visitors to Johns's studio, one of whom remarked that she found the paintings empty and without meaning, as if he had painted what he saw out of his window, a view of a vacant parking lot. Johns turned the irony of this comment into the title of the painting.

The one hundred and forty-four works offered from the estate of Robert C. Scull comprised the balance of the collection, ranging from works by Abstract Expressionists such as Franz Kline to those by Neil Jenney, Bruce Nauman (Fig. 2), and others who were unknown when the Sculls bought them in the late 1960s and early '70s. The group included seminal works by Pop artists, among them James Rosenquist's *F111* (Fig. 3). Begun in 1964, the painting was designed to cover all four walls of the Castelli Gallery, where it was exhibited the following year. On the last day of the show, as the artist and dealer prepared to dismantle the painting to sell the panels individually, Scull arrived and purchased the work in its entirety. Its size and overt political content generated public and critical comment in 1965 and again last autumn during the Rosenquist retrospective at the Whitney Museum of American Art. The original idea stemmed from a visit to a Texas amusement park where the latest fighter bomber, the F111, was displayed on the grass. In the painting, the bomber becomes a menacing backdrop for images of recreation and the life of post-war America.

George Segal's *Portrait of Robert and Ethel Scull* depicted the couple in their heyday as contemporary art collectors. Although Segal discouraged portrait commissions, he made exceptions for certain collectors, among them Vera List and the Sculls. Executed in 1965, the portrait was intended to reflect the lives of the sitters and their aspirations; the blank red canvas was, of course a reference to their collection. According to Segal, being portrayed 'is putting on one's best face and clothes' so Bob went on a diet and Ethel wore her best Courrèges boots (which remained inside the sculpture) and had her hair done by Kenneth for the occasion. Tellingly, this image of the American Pop movement's most famous collectors was purchased for a record $137,000 by a Japanese collector.

The Scull collections have now been dispersed but the influence of Robert and Ethel Scull will continue to be felt in the contemporary field as works they once owned enter museum collections and appear on the auction market. This phenomenon has already been evident, particularly in the auction of de Kooning's *Woman*, 1953, (Fig. 4), which was offered unsuccessfully in the 1965 Scull sale and sold for $2,530,000 in May of this year.

Fig. 4
Willem de Kooning
WOMAN
Oil on paper laid down on canvas, signed, 1953, 31in by 22in (78.7cm by 55.9cm)
New York $2,530,000 (£1,505,952). 4.V.87
From the Playboy Enterprises Corporate Collection

John James Audubon

A PAIR OF BOAT-TAILED GRACKLES

Watercolour, pen and ink, pastel, graphite and egg wash on paper, mounted on board, inscribed in an engraver's hand *Drawn by John J. Audubon from Nature*, 1824, 10½in by 14 in (26.7cm by 35.6cm)

New York $253,000 (£155,213). 28.V.87

A version of this watercolour appeared in the four-volume supplement to Alexander Wilson's *American Ornithology*, and represents the significant starting point of Audubon's career as an illustrator of natural history subjects.

Rembrandt Peale
PORTRAIT OF FRANKLIN PEALE — BOY BLOWING A BUBBLE
1808, 30in by 25in (76.2cm by 63.5cm)
New York $418,000 (£256,442). 28.V.87
From the collection of the late Suzanne Colton Wilson

John Haberle
IMITATION
Signed and dated *New Haven, Ct., 1887,* and signed on a clipping painted on the frame,
10in by 14in (25.4cm by 35.5cm)
New York $517,000 (£317,178). 28.V.87
From the collection of Mr and Mrs Peter L. Chapman

This work, which signalled the most important phase in Haberle's career as a *trompe l'oeil* artist, was exhibited at the National Academy of Design in 1887 and was immediately bought by Thomas Clarke, a noted collector, who wrote to a New York dealer in 1888: 'In my collection I have the *Imitation* which created so much talk in the National Academy of Design last fall. I regard the work of Mr Haberle as remarkable and curious . . . W.M. Harnett the still life painter studied the picture named, and said that he had never seen such reproduction anywhere.'

Opposite
Thomas Eakins
THE ART STUDENT — PORTRAIT OF JAMES WRIGHT
Signed and dated *1890,* and signed with the artist's initials on the reverse,
42in by 32in (106.7cm by 81.3cm)
New York $2,420,000 (£1,484,663). 28.V.87
From the collection of Caroline Ryan Foulke

Winslow Homer

IN CHARGE OF BABY

Watercolour, signed and dated *'73*, also signed and dated beneath the mat, sight: 8½in by 13½in
(21.6cm by 34.3cm): size overall: 9½in by 13½in (24.1cm by 34.3cm)
New York $770,000 (£472,393). 28.V.87
From the collection of Caroline Ryan Foulke

Opposite
James Abbott McNeill Whistler

VARIATIONS IN VIOLET AND GREEN

Signed with butterfly on a cartouche and dated *'71*, and signed with a butterfly and dated *1871* on
the frame, 24in by 14in (61cm by 35.5cm)
New York $2,585,000 (£1,585,890). 28.V.87
From the collection of Caroline Ryan Foulke

Theodore Robinson
SUMMER HILLSIDE, GIVERNY
Circa 1889, 18in by 24in (45.7cm by 61cm)
New York $522,500 (365,385). 4.XII.86

Opposite
Mary Cassatt
LOUISE ALLAITANT SON ENFANT
Pastel, signed, 1899, 28½in by 21in (72.4cm by 53.4cm)
London £990,000 ($1,435,500). 2.XII.86

Albert Bierstadt
YOSEMITE
Signed, 20in by 28¼in (50.8cm by 71.7cm)
New York $550,000 (£337,423). 28.V.87

Frederick Frieseke
ON THE RIVER
Signed and titled on a label on the stretcher, *circa* 1909–10,
26in by 32in (66cm by 81.3cm)
New York $319,000 (£223,077). 4.XII. 86

Rufino Tamayo
WOMEN OF TEHUANTEPEC
Gouache on canvas, signed and dated *39*, 5in by 7⅛in (12.7cm by 18cm)
New York $46,200 (£27,500). 19.V.87

Fernando Botero
THE BASHFUL FAMILY
Signed and dated *68*, also signed, titled and dated on the reverse,
79⅛in by 71¼in (201cm by 181cm)
New York $148,500 (£103,846). 25.XI.86

Wifredo Lam
FEMME CHEVAL
Signed, 1954, 50½in by 37¾in (128.3cm by 95.9cm)
New York $110,000 (£65,476). 19.V.87

Matta
SOTTOBOSCO
Signed and dated *52*, 47¼in by 79½in (120cm by 202cm)
New York $165,000 (£98,214). 19.V.87

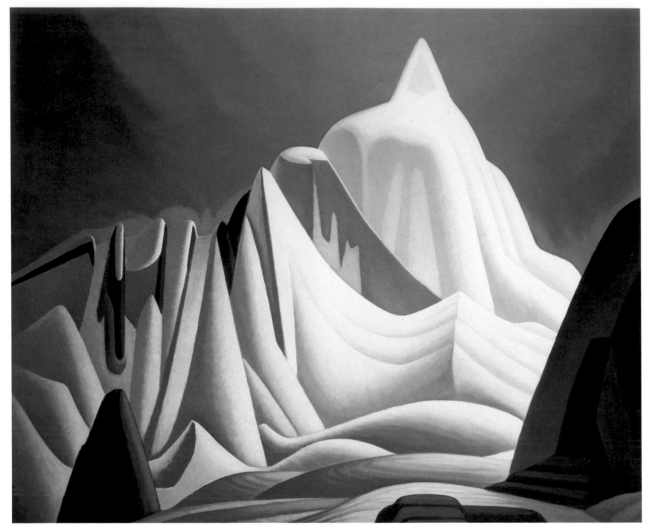

Lawren Stewart Harris
MOUNTAINS IN SNOW: ROCKY MOUNTAIN PAINTINGS, NO.VII
Circa 1929, titled by the artist on the stretcher and on a label on the reverse,
51in by 58in (129.5cm by 147.3cm)
Toronto Can$495,000 (£255,155:$356,115). 18.XI.86

Opposite
Antoine Toussaint de Chazal
PORTRAIT OF CAPTAIN MATTHEW FLINDERS, R.N.
25⅜in by 19¾in (64.5cm by 50cm)
Melbourne $451,000 (£197,807:$322,143). 6.IV.87

Captain Matthew Flinders' place in Australian history is assured: an hydrographer and explorer,
he was the first man to circumnavigate the continent from 1801–1803, and the first to refer
consistently to the land as 'Australia'.

Photographs

Margaret Bourke-White
AIRSHIP AKRON, WINNER OF THE GOODYEAR ZEPPELIN RACE
Silver print, signed by the photographer in ink on the image, framed in duralumin used in the girder construction of the airship, and inscribed *Winner Sanford Tire Shop Third Annual Goodyear Dealers Zeppelin Race July-August 1931*, 17$\frac{1}{4}$in by 23in (43.9cm by 58.5cm)
New York $24,200 (£14,320). 6.V.87

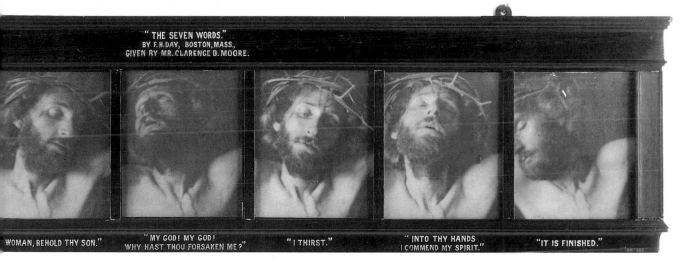

Above

F. Holland Day

THE SEVEN WORDS

A series of seven platinum prints, mounted on
card and numbered on the reverse in an
unidentified hand, in the original frame, with
remnants of the exhibition label from the
Philadelphia Photography Salon, signed,
titled and inscribed by the photographer
in ink on the reverse, 1898,
each print 5¼in by 4¼in (13.3cm by 10.8cm)
New York $93,500 (£64,931). 10.XI.86

Right

David Hockney

THE BROOKLYN BRIDGE

Photocollage of Kodacolour prints, signed,
titled, dated and numbered *15* by the
photographer in ink on the mount, from an
edition of 20, 1982, sheet size 108in by 57½in
(274.5cm by 146cm)
New York $38,500 (£22,781). 6.V.87

Dr John Murray
THE TAJ MAHAL FROM THE EAST
Albumen print and a waxed paper negative, late 1850s, 14½in by 18⅛in
(37cm by 46cm)
London £7,700 ($11,396). 31.X.86

Robert Howlett
ISAMBARD KINGDOM BRUNEL STANDING BEFORE THE LAUNCHING CHAINS OF 'THE LEVIATHAN',
('THE GREAT EASTERN')
Albumen print, 1857, 10¼in by 8in (25.9cm by 20.2cm)
London £22,000 ($38,720). 1.V.87

Prints

Albrecht Dürer
ADAM AND EVE
Engraving, Meder IIb, dated *1504*, 9$\frac{7}{8}$in by 7$\frac{5}{8}$in (25cm by 19.4cm)
London £242,000 ($365,420). 1.XII.86

Albrecht Dürer
MELENCOLIA
Engraving, Meder IIa, dated *1514*, 9½in by 7½in (24.1cm by 18.9cm)
New York $511,500 (£306,287). 13.V.87
From the collection of the Kimbell Art Foundation, Fort Worth, Texas

Rembrandt Harmensz. van Rijn
FAUST
Etching and drypoint, on oatmeal paper, the first state of three, $8\frac{1}{4}$in by $6\frac{1}{4}$in (21cm by 15.9cm)
London £209,000 ($355,300). 29.VI.87
From the collection of the British Rail Pension Funds

Francisco Jose de Goya y Lucientes
'¡QUAL LA DESCANOAN!', PLATE 21 OF 'LOS CAPRICHOS'
Etching and aquatint, $8\frac{1}{2}$in by $5\frac{3}{4}$in (21.6cm by 14.6cm)
London £79,200 ($134,640). 29.VI.87
From the collection of the British Rail Pension Funds

This is the only recorded working proof before engraved letters and numbers.

Edgar Degas

AUTOPORTRAIT

Etching with drypoint, signed in black chalk and dedicated *à Bartholomé*, one of only eight
known impressions of the third state, 1857, 9in by 5⅝in (23cm by 14.4cm)
New York $203,500 (£121,856). 13.V.87
From the collection of the Kimbell Art Foundation, Fort Worth, Texas

Opposite
Mary Cassatt

THE LETTER

Colour, drypoint, soft ground and aquatint, signed in pencil and inscribed *Edition de 25
épreuves Imprimé par l'artiste et M Leroy, circa* 1891, sheet size 13⅝in by 8¾in (34.6cm by 22.3cm)
New York $192,500 (£115,269). 13.V.87
From the collection of the late Flora Whitney Miller

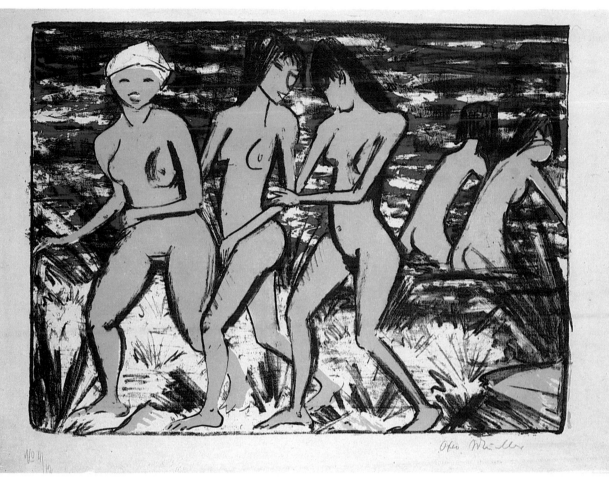

Otto Mueller
FÜNF GELBE AKTE AM WASSER
Lithograph printed in colours, on Japan laid paper, signed in pencil and numbered *4/12*, 1921,
sheet size approximately 13⅛in by 17¼in (33.3cm by 43.7cm)
London £22,000 ($37,400). 30.VI.87

Opposite
Edvard Munch
MADONNA – LIEBENDES WEIB
Hand-coloured lithograph, on Japan paper mounted on card, inscribed in pencil by the artist
'*Til Jappe fra Munch*, 1895, 23¾in by 17¼in (60.5cm by 44cm)
New York $253,000 (£151,497). 14.V.87
From the collection of the Kimbell Art Foundation, Fort Worth, Texas

Jappe Nilssen, to whom this impression is dedicated, was a distinguished art critic and an early
supporter of the artist.

Christopher Richard Wynne Nevinson
BUILDING AIRCRAFT
One of a set of six lithographs, signed in pencil, numbered *21* from the edition
of 200 and dated *1917*, published by the Stationery Office as part of the series
The Great War: Britain's Efforts and Ideals,
sheet size 15¼in by 19⅞in (38.5cm by 50.5cm)
London £22,000 ($37,400). 29.VI.87

Opposite
Henri Matisse
JAZZ
Two in a book of twenty stencils, printed in colours, after collages and cut paper
designs, with facsimile manuscript text by the artist, signed in pencil and numbered
203 from the edition of 250, published by Tériade, Paris, 1947
New York $132,000 (£79,042). 13.V.87
From the collection of the Kimbell Art Foundation, Fort Worth, Texas

Jasper Johns
COLOUR NUMERALS: FIGURES FROM 0–9
Number *7* of a set of ten lithographs printed in colours, on Japanese Arjomari paper, each signed
in a different colour crayon, dated and numbered *16/40*, 1968–69, sheet size approximately
38in by 31in (96.5cm by 78.7cm)
New York $154,000 (£108,451). 22.XI.86

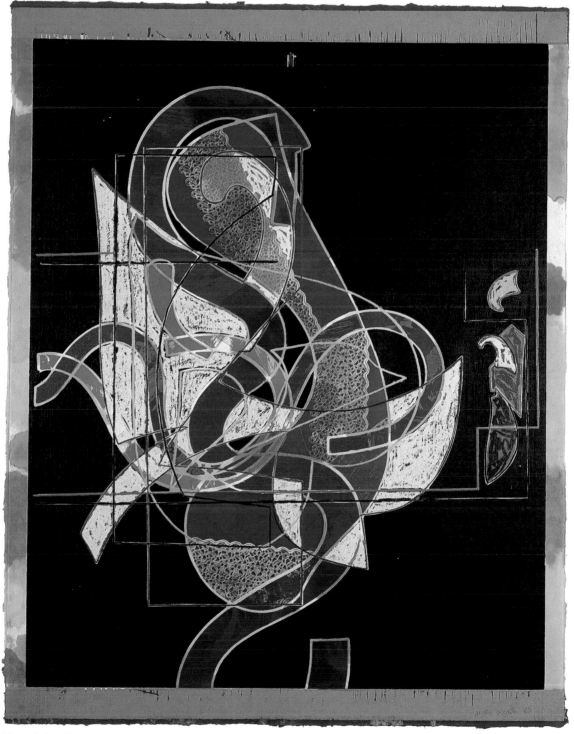

Frank Stella
CIRCUITS: PERGUSA THREE
Relief-printed etching and woodcut printed in colours, on dyed handmade paper, signed in pencil, dated *'83* and inscribed *A.P.X.*, one of ten artist's proofs, aside from the numbered edition of thirty, sheet size 66⅞in by 52in (170cm by 132cm)
New York $88,000 (£52,695). 15.V.87

Printed books, autograph letters and manuscripts

Biblia Pauperum, a fifteenth-century block book with Latin text, thirty-seven leaves arranged in single sheets of two leaves each, printed on one side only from a double woodblock, North Netherlands, *circa* 1460
London £148,500 ($222,750). 27.XI.86
From the collection of His Grace the Duke of Northumberland, KG, GCVO, TD, PC

The woodcuts depicting scenes from the life of Christ with Old Testament prefigurations and prophecies were intended to instruct the poor and illiterate. In style, they are reminiscent of the Flemish school of the late fourteenth century, and are possibly after drawings that have been ascribed to Roger van der Weyden (1390–1464).

Right
Clement of Alexandria, edited by Piero Vettori, first edition, Edward VI's copy with a contemporary London binding by the 'Medallion Binder', calf gilt, Lorenzo Torrentino, Florence, 1550
London £71,500 ($121,550). 24.VII.87
From the collection of Elizabeth, Dowager Duchess of Manchester

auy tost quil le pouira et quil ensera requis en foy de quoy les dits sieurs commissaires et Ambassadeur ont signé le present traicté et a iceluy fait apposer le cachet de leurs armes. a Douures ce vingt et deuxiesme jour du mois de may lán de grace mil six cens soixante et dix.

Arlington
H Arundel
J Clifford
R Bellings

Charles R.

Charles par la grace de dieu Roy de la Grande Bretagne France et Irelande defenseur de la foy, a tous ceux qui ces presentes lettres verront Salut. ayans leu et meurement considéré les pouuoirs du sieur Colbert Ambassadeur de nostre tres cher et tres amé frere et cousin le Roy treschrestien datés du 31 d'octobre 1669 par les quels nostre dit frere luy donne autorité de conferer auec les commissaires que nous pourrions nommer, traitter, conclurre, et signer des articles d'une plus estroite amitie, liaison, et confederation entre nous, et declare que nulle autre alliance ne luy peut estre plus agreable ny plus auantageuse a ses sujets; nous qui sommes dans les mesmes dispositions, et qui n'auons point de desir plus ardent que de nous lier d'une amitie par faire et indissoluble auec nostre dit frere, y estant conuiés et par la proximité du sang, l'affection et estime que nous auons

pour

The Secret Treaty of Dover, 1670, a collection of working drafts, memoranda, correspondence and agreements secretly preserved in the archive of Thomas, first Lord Clifford of Chudleigh (1630-73), Lord High Treasurer of England, concerning the negotiations for the Treaty, including signed protocols for the final ratified version, approximately 320 pages
London £313,500 ($514,140). 24.VII.87
From the collection of the thirteenth Lord Clifford of Chudleigh

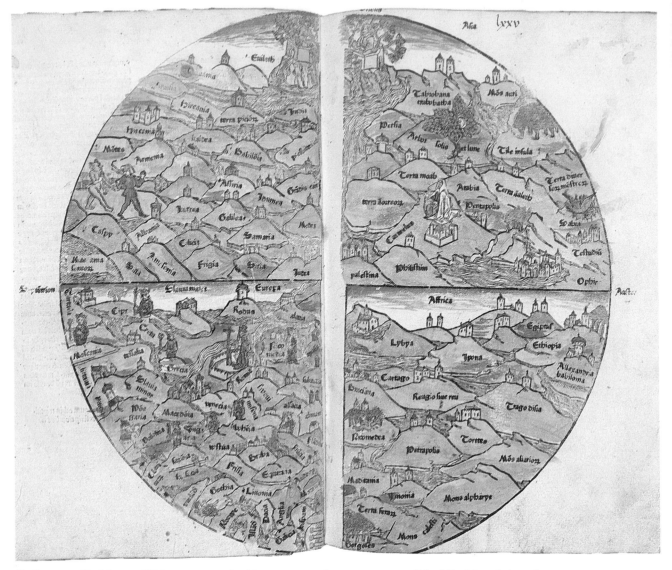

Rudimentum Novitiorum, 473 leaves, two double-page woodcut maps, one of the World and the other of Palestine, a view of Jerusalem, further maps and numerous genealogical tables and woodcut illustrations in the text, fully coloured in a contemporary hand, Lucas Brandis de Schass, Lübeck, 5 August 1475
London £55,000 ($93,500). 26.VI.87

Opposite, above
Johannes Blaeu
Le Grand Atlas (*Atlas Major*) or *Cosmographie Blaviane*, twelve volumes, second French text edition, with 599 engraved maps, plans, views and plates by Willem and Johannes Blaeu, augmented by an additional twenty-one double-page maps by Nicolaes Visscher and Frederick de Wit, Johannes Blaeu, Amsterdam, 1667
London £110,000 ($166,100). 23.X.86

Below
Henry Chamberlain
Views and Costumes of the City and Neighbourhood of Rio de Janiero, first edition, thirty-five coloured aquatints including five folding panoramas by Henry Alken, John Clarke, T. and G. Hunt after Chamberlain, 1822
London £48,400 ($82,280). 25.VI.87

Botanical colour-plate books from the library of Robert de Belder

Roy Davids

Robert de Belder, one of the most distinguished figures in the horticultural world, enjoyed both the means and the knowledge to assemble an unrivalled private library entirely devoted to botany, from which examples of colour-plate books spanning the period from 1600 to 1900 were selected for auction at Sotheby's in April 1987. To M. de Belder the books were never merely an antiquarian pursuit, but related to the development of his arboretum at Kalmthout in Belgium, a conspicuous feature of the European horticultural landscape.

Until the end of the sixteenth century botanical illustration was primarily occupied with providing aids for the identification of medicinal samples. At the beginning of the seventeenth century an aesthetic revolution took place, coinciding with an expansion of trade, which led to the importation of exotic species into Europe. The documentation of this enlargement of the floral kingdom gave birth to the science of plant classification in its own right, and to the first sumptuously produced florilegia, celebrating private gardens and their treasures.

Among the early florilegia in the sale was, first and foremost, Besler's *Hortus eystettensis* (see opposite) and a superb copy of Daniel Rabel's *Theatrum florae* (see p. 190). Indeed, the fine state of many of the books in this collection received recognition far beyond normal expectations. This resulted, for instance, in the astonishing price paid for Thornton's *Temple of Flora* (see p. 190), excellent copies of which have not previously exceeded £50,000.

The eighteenth and nineteenth centuries witnessed a flood of botanical books, reaching an apogee with Georg Dionysius Ehret's illustrations for Trew's *Plantae selectae* (£99,000: $173,250) and *Hortus nitidissimus* (see p. 190), a superb copy, which made more than four times the sum expected before the sale. With the nineteenth century came the advent of a new technique in botanical art: the lithographed plate, coloured by hand. Wallich's *Plantae Asiaticae rariores* (£16,500: $28,875) and Martius's *Historia naturalis palmarum* (£25,300: $44,275) are just two examples from the de Belder collection demonstrating that there was no decline in artistic excellence in the new medium.

In the annals of Sotheby's, which began with a book sale in 1744, the sale of the library of Robert de Belder, which realized £5.9 million ($10.3 million), will rank as one of the most memorable. The lavishly illustrated catalogue is in itself an invaluable work of reference and source of delight.

Basilius Besler
Hortus eystettensis, first edition, one volume bound in two, 367 engraved plates of flowers
and plants on 368 sheets with contemporary colouring, Konrad Bauer, Altdorf, 1613
London £605,000 ($1,064,800). 27.IV.87

Above, left
Daniel Rabel
Theatrum florae, first edition, engraved title and
frontispiece and 69 plates from drawings by
Rabel, with contemporary hand-colouring signed
and dated *1624* by the artist William Theodore,
N. de Mathonière, Paris, 1622
London £187,000 ($327,250). 28.IV.87

Above, right
Robert John Thornton
*New Illustration of the Sexual System of Carolus von
Linnaeus. . . . The Temple of Flora, or Garden of Nature,*
31 colour-printed aquatint and mezzotint plates,
finished by hand, in a contemporary diced russia
and gilt binding, 1799–1807
London £187,000 ($327,250). 28.IV.87

Right
Christoph Jakob Trew
Hortus nitidissimus omnem per annum superbiens floribus,
first edition, three volumes in one, 180 hand-
coloured engraved plates, forty-four contributed
by Ehret, Seligmann, Nuremberg, 1750–86
London £308,000 ($539,000). 28.IV.87

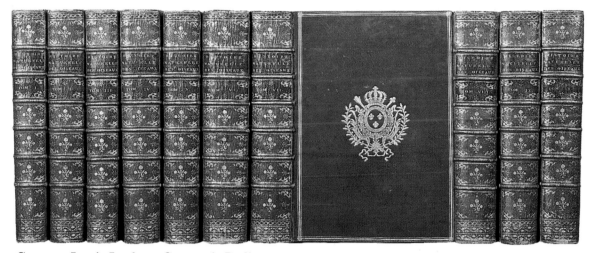

Georges Louis Leclerc, Comte de Buffon
Histoire naturelle des Oiseaux, ten volumes, 966 (of 973) hand-coloured etched plates by F.N. Martinet
and others under the supervision of E.L. Daubenton, in a contemporary red morocco and gilt
binding, stamped with the arms of Louis XV, Imprimerie Royale, Paris, 1771–1786
London £55,000 ($93,500). 25.VI.87

John Gould
The author's imperial
folio collection of his own
works, sold individually,
containing 3,265 hand-
coloured lithographed
plates, the complete
works bound in
contemporary full or half
green morocco, 1831–88,
the plate illustrated is
from *The Birds of Europe*
London £397,485
($683,674). 23.IV.87

Thomas Lewin
Drawings of Birds, 143 original watercolour drawings painted life size after specimens in
English collections, including birds from North, South and Central America, India and Africa,
all but four signed, unpublished, London, 1825–31
New York $82,500 (£50,613). 18.VI.87

Above
Charles Edward Brock
The complete set of twenty-four ink and
watercolour drawings for Jane Austen's *Emma*,
comprising ornamental title-page and
twenty-three full-page illustrations, the latter
signed and dated *1909*
London £46,200 ($78,540). 19.VI.87

Above, left
Charles Folkard
The Land of Nursery Rhyme, nineteen drawings,
including eight large watercolour and gouache
designs illustrating the volume compiled by
Alice Daglish and Ernst Rhys, 1932
London £26,400 ($44,880). 19.VI.87

Left
Aubrey Beardsley
The Achieving of the Sangreal, and ink and wash
drawing signed with device, for the frontispiece
to Malory's *Le Morte Darthur* volume 2, 1893–94
London £104,500 ($177,650). 19.VI.87

An unknown autograph manuscript of Mozart's symphonies

Stephen Roe

Mozart's position in the first rank of symphonists is indisputable. It might be thought, then, that all the autograph manuscripts of these works would be in major libraries in Austria, Germany and America. In late 1986 I was invited to inspect a manuscript of 'a Mozart symphony' and found in the small volume placed before me the autograph manuscript of not one, but nine symphonies (nos. 22–30, K.162, 181–84 and 199–202). All the scores were in perfect condition, as if Mozart had just laid down his pen.

The manuscript can only be described in superlatives: it is undoubtedly the most important music manuscript offered for sale at auction this century, containing nearly one quarter of the numbered symphonies of Mozart. It is the primary source and the only surviving autograph full score of the symphonies and the largest autograph manuscript of Mozart in private hands. It could be said that it is the most important musical manuscript by any composer outside public collections.

Some of the greatest works written by Mozart during the 1770s are in this volume, including at least three masterpieces: the symphonies in G minor, no.25 (K.183), C major, no.28 (K.200) and the A major, no.29 (K.201), the last-mentioned (Fig. 1) possibly the most original and assured work written by Mozart in that decade and described by Jens Peter Larsen as 'the crowning achievement of Mozart's early symphonies'. These three symphonies mark the emergence of the composer from a preternaturally gifted youth to a composer of maturity, exhibiting the same perfection as the final triad of 1788 [nos. 39–41, K.543, 550 and 551], though on a lower rung of the ladder and within narrower limits' (A. Einstein, *Mozart*, 1971). The other six works, though written on a smaller scale (five being in three rather than four movements), contain much fine music.

We have to thank Leopold Mozart for the survival of this collection. It was he who preserved the nine works by assembling the separate manuscripts, making a correction or annotation here and there, and providing an introductory contents page in which all the works are listed with incipits of the first movements and details of the orchestration meticulously supplied. The volume contains 508 pages (including blanks), the majority of which are in Mozart's hand with six autograph titles (Figs. 1 and 2). The first movement of the symphony in E flat (K.184) is an exception: the first two pages are transcribed by Mozart's father Leopold and the rest of the movement is in the hand of an anonymous Salzburg scribe. An example

Fig. 1
Wolfgang Amadeus Mozart
An autograph page of the opening of symphony no. 29 from a volume containing the manuscript
score of nine symphonies, 508 pages, the majority in the composer's hand, one movement and
annotations in the hands of Leopold Mozart and a copyist, *circa* 1773–74
London £2,585,000 ($4,575,450). 22.V.87

of the paternal piety lavished on this volume is evident at the opening of symphony
no.24 in B flat (K.182). At the head of the score Mozart wrote the title and signed
his name: *Sinfonia . . . Wolfgango Amadeo Mozart . . . .* His father, ever solicitous for
his son's reputation, inserted the words *Del Sigr. Cavaliere* before the signature,
making reference to the title of the Order of the Golden Spur awarded to the
fourteen-year-old composer by the Pope in 1770.

The manuscript bears some traces of later ownership. The blue-grey outer
wrappers are inscribed by Leopold von Sonnleithner, the friend of Beethoven and
Schubert, who was the first recorded owner of the manuscript outside Mozart's
circle. The next owner, the Leipzig music-publisher August Cranz, may have been
responsible for the printer's markings on some of the symphonies. After Cranz, the
volume passed into obscurity until its emergence at Sotheby's. There is considerable
evidence to suggest that these are 'composing scores', not merely fair copies bound
together and preserved by Leopold. While the writing is, on the whole, remarkably
neat, there are occasional deletions and cancelled drafts of small sections, for

Fig. 2
An autograph page of the opening of symphony no. 23, inscribed *Sinfonia . . . di Wolfgango Mozart*

example in the first movement of K.162 and, significantly, in the first two bars of the slow movement of the G minor symphony where there is a false start.

The symphonies were probably composed between 1773 and 1774, after the Mozart family's return from their third and last trip to Italy. Curiously, all the dates on the scores have been deleted, seemingly not by Mozart himself, but certainly by a contemporary hand. The reason for this can only be a matter for speculation. It has been thought that Mozart, in an attempt to have the works performed in Vienna in the 1780s, may have been trying to disguise that they were ten years old. In an age in which novelty was important, the fact that these works were composed in Mozart's youth in Salzburg, may have been a negative factor for performance in the sophisticated capital of Vienna. Now, following the sale, the manuscript is again in private hands, but we understand that it will be on loan to the Pierpont Morgan Library, New York. In addition to the two symphonies of Mozart already in the library, we believe the acquisition of this manuscript makes the library the largest repository of autograph manuscripts of symphonies by the composer. Thus for the first time in over two hundred years, this extraordinary volume has found a resting place in a public collection.

Gustav Mahler
The autograph full-score of the composer's first major song cycle, *'Lieder eines fahrenden Gesellen'*, with many differences from the published versions, fifty-eight pages, 1891–93
London £198,000 ($298,980). 28.XI.86

William Shakespeare
An Elizabethan manuscript
notebook containing
memorized extracts from
Henry IV, Part I, the earliest
known quotations of any
consequence from the play,
predating publication in 1598,
circa 1594
London £165,000 ($247,500).
18.XII.86

The Popish Plot, a collection
of fourteen hundred broadsides
and pamphlets relating to the
alleged Popish plot, arranged
and indexed in thirteen
volumes, including material
relating to a number of trials
(some before Judge Jeffreys),
comprising popular verses,
ballads, songs, satirical
allegories, elegies,
proclamations, scaffold
statements and wills,
annotated throughout in the
same hand, 1660–95
London £110,000 ($187,000).
24.VII.87

William Butler Yeats
An autograph manuscript book, bound in
vellum, eight pages containing seven
poems, one unpublished, with pencil titles
of twelve further poems on the following
leaves, the preliminary leaf inscribed twice
by Yeats *To Miss Maud Gonne from WB
Yeats. October 20 1891*
London £34,100 ($57,970). 23.VII.87

Sir   Monticello May 28.18.

I thank you for the Discourse on the consecration of the Synagogue in your city, with which you have been pleased to favor me. I have read it with pleasure and instruction, having learnt from it some valuable facts in Jewish history which I did not know before. your sect has furnished *by it's sufferings* a remarkable proof of the universal spirit of *religious* intolerance, inherent in every sect, disclaimed by all while feeble, and practised by all when in power. our laws have applied the only antidote to this vice, protecting our religious, as they do our civil rights by putting all on an equal footing. but more remains to be done. for altho' we are free by the law, we are not so in practice. public opinion erects itself into an Inquisition, and exercises it's office with as much fanaticism as fans the flames of an Auto da fé. the prejudice still scowling on your section of our religion, altho' the elder one, cannot be unfelt by yourselves. it is to be hoped that individual dispositions will at length mould themselves to the model of the law, and consider the moral basis on which all our religions rest, as the rallying point which unites them in a common interest; while the peculiar dogmas branching from it are the exclusive concern of the respective sects embracing them, and no rightful subject of notice to any other. public opinion needs reformation on this point, which would have the further happy effect of doing away the hypocritical maxim of 'intus ut lubet, foris ut moris.' nothing I think would be so likely to effect this as to your sect particularly as the more careful attention to education, which you recommend, and which placing it's members on the equal and commanding benches of science, will exhibit them as equal objects of respect and favor. I should not do full justice to the merits of your discourse, were I not, in addition to that of it's matter, to express my consideration of it as a fine specimen of style & composition. I salute you with great respect and esteem.

                                                Th:Jefferson

Thomas Jefferson
An autograph letter to Mordecai M. Noah, in response to the gift of a pamphlet printing of Noah's speech given at the consecration of the Synagogue Shearith Israel in New York on 17 April 1818, signed and dated *Monticello May 28.18*
New York $396,000 (£280,851). 29.X.86
From the collection of the late Charles J. Rosenbloom

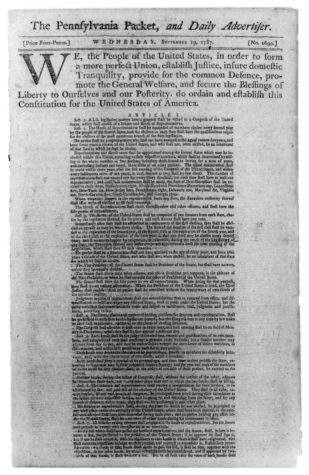

Above

Franz Kafka

A collection of letters from Franz Kafka
to his fiancée Felice Bauer comprising
327 autograph letters, 15 typed letters,
145 autograph postcards, 33 typed
postcards and 5 telegrams, dated from
20 September 1912 to 16 October 1917
New York $605,000 (£371,165).
18.VI.87
From the collection of Schocken Books, Inc.

Right

The first authorized publication of the
Constitution of the United States in the
Pennsylvania Packet, and Daily Advertiser,
No. 2690, Philadelphia,
Wednesday, September 19, 1787
New York $110,000 (£65,868). 13.V.87

Samuel Langhorne Clemens (Mark Twain)
'The $30,000 Bequest', the original autograph manuscript, 81 leaves with numerous holograph emendations, corrections and deletions, Florence, 1903
New York $110,000 (£67,485). 18.VI.87
Property from the library of the Col. Richard Gimbel family

Manuscripts

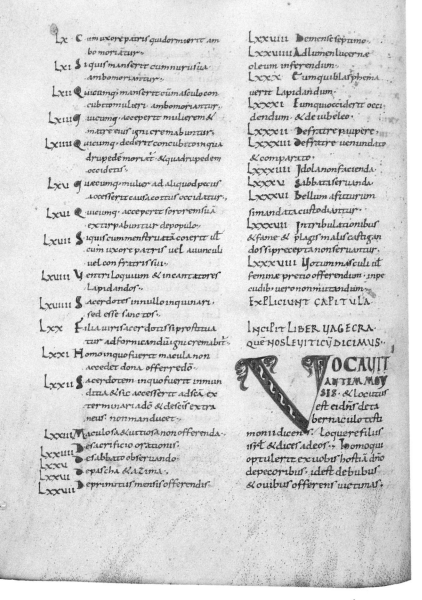

The Bible of Santa Cecilia, one of seven large decorated initials in a Latin
manuscript on vellum, volume I of two volumes, Rome, late ninth century
London £231,000 ($390,390). 23.VI.87
From the collection of the Brooklyn Museum

Opposite
The Armagnac Breviary, one of forty-seven miniatures in a Latin manuscript on
vellum, written and illuminated for Jean de Roussay, Chamberlain to the
Duc d'Orléans, Paris, *circa* 1400
London £704,000 ($1,189,760). 23.VI.87

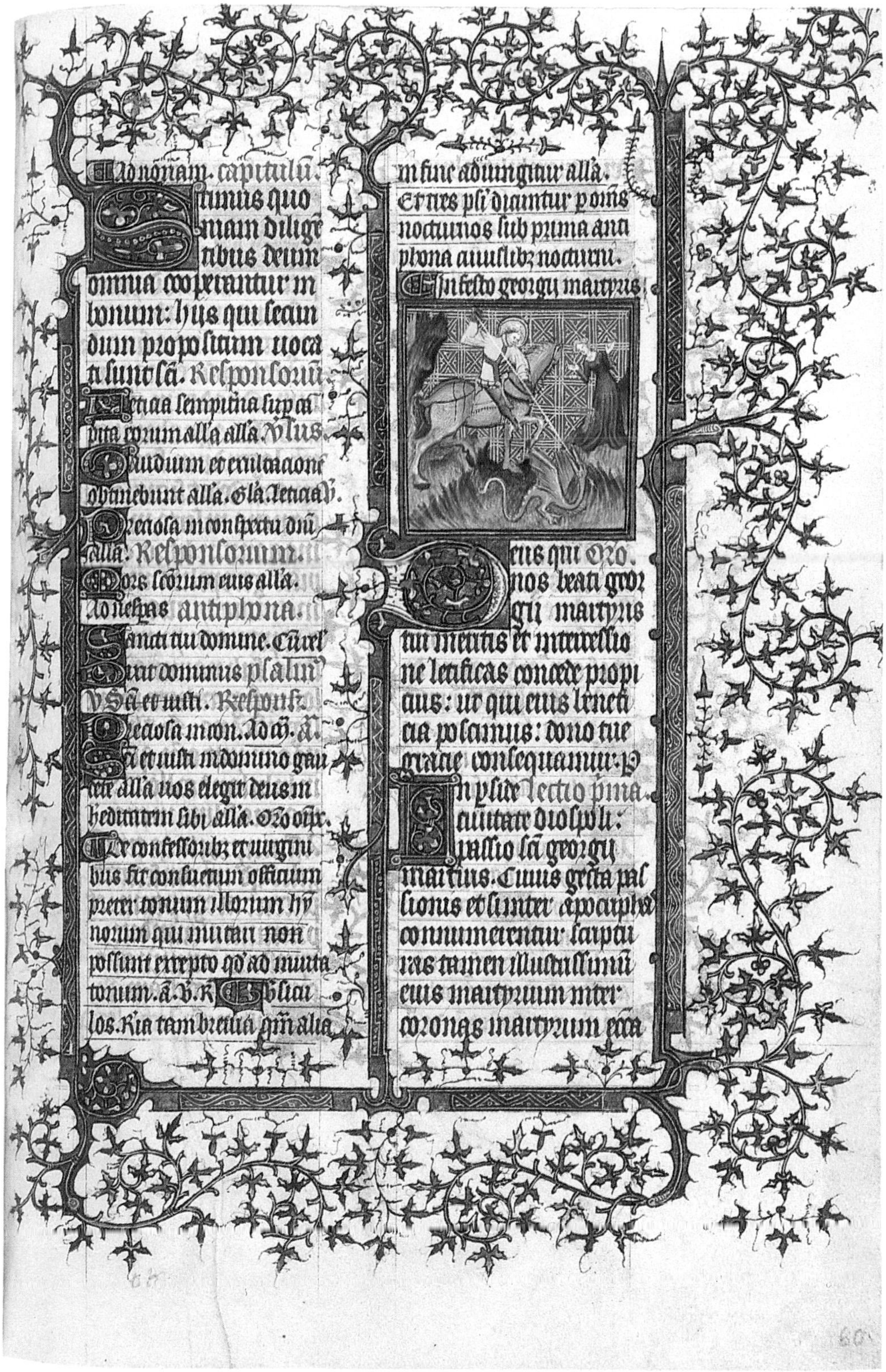

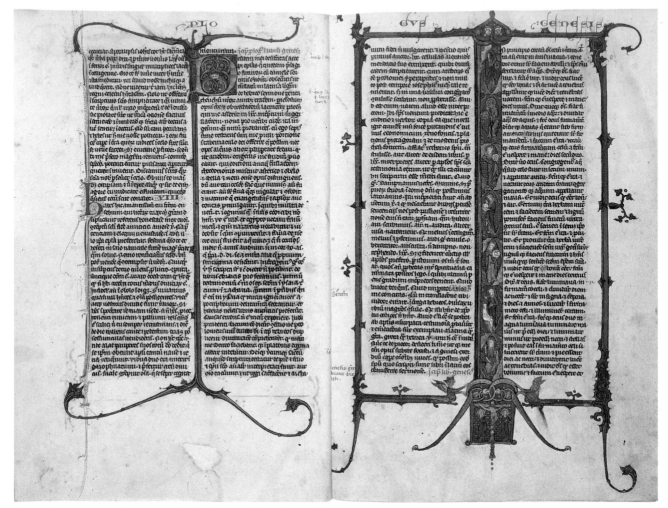

One of eighty-four historiated initials in an illuminated Latin manuscript Bible on vellum,
Normandy, *circa* 1300
London £176,000 ($265,760). 2.XII.86

This was the eighth time that this manuscript has been sold at Sotheby's since 1745.

Opposite
Gaston Phébus
Livre de Chasse, one of eighty-six miniatures in an illuminated manuscript on vellum,
Brittany, *circa* 1430
Monaco FF7,564,000 (£804,681:$1,244,079). 28.II.87
From the collection of the late Marcel Jeanson

t se leueue
ur uenlt
chaaer le
dam il le doit
queur tout
ainsi que
iay dit du rangier de quatre ou
de vi. chiens au plus hault les
plus saiges et les meilleurs qil
ait. Et se les chiens tieu
uent ou il euua viande au ma
tin ou de la releuee de la nuit il
leur doit laissier faire et attend
et non pas trop haster iucques
atant quilz le facent sailly et

mettre pie a terre et regaudr q
ses chiens ne aillent la contre
ongle. Et duek le chaaer
tout ainsi que iay dit du cerk.
Car vn dain fuit tout ainsi
comme fait vn cerf fors tant
qul fuit plus longuement
et les vuees que ne fait le cerf
et plus longuement fuit a
necques le change et plus
souuent ressaut aux chiens.
Si le doit chaaer re
chaaer relaissier et requeur
ainsi que iay dit du cerf et
les courher et le deffaire tout

The young Abd-ur-Rahim Khan presented to the emperor Akbar in 1561, attributed to Sur Das, an illustrated leaf from the *Akbarnama*, Mughal, *circa* 1604
New York $47,300 (£29,379).
25.III.87

Opposite
A portrait of Selim III, one of thirty-two portraits from a biographical treatise on the Sultans of Turkey, Ottoman, nineteenth century
London £18,700 ($27,863). 20.XI.86

Works of art

A French Gothic limestone group of
the Virgin and Child, possibly
Tournai, formerly in the Abbey of
Fontenay, late fourteenth century,
height 76¾in(195cm)
Monte Carlo FF1,720,500
(£172,050:$286,750). 22.VI.87

An early Christian ivory pyxis

Archer St Clair

The discovery of a previously unknown ivory pyxis is an unexpected and important event for the history of ivory carving. The pyxis (Figs 1–4), which came to light as the sleeve of a nineteenth-century French tankard, is one of the largest of its type that survives, its diameter exceeded only by that of the so-called 'Great Berlin' pyxis. Its lid and bottom are lost, but with the exception of a vertical crack beneath the lock space and numerous drilled holes in the lock and hinge spaces, the pyxis is in very good condition.

Approximately forty ivory pyxides decorated with Christian scenes survive from the early Christian period. Reflecting the size and shape of the tusk from which they are cut, these boxes are round or oval, and were supplied with a separate bottom and lid, which surviving examples indicate were also of ivory. Most have a lock space for the attachment of a metal lock. Hinge spaces are less common, and many pyxides bear the marks of hinges attached with little regard for the carved images they obliterate. On this pyxis the lock space has been largely cut away (Fig. 1). There are two hinge spaces opposite (Fig. 4). The area between them has been recut, interrupting the architectural setting. The large hinge spaces that interrupt the biblical scenes (Figs 2 and 3), and the number *1501* incised beneath the lock space (Fig. 1) appear to be later additions as well, probably reflecting a remounting.

Used in the middle ages primarily as reliquaries or as containers for incense, it has been suggested that these pyxides were created as containers for the eucharistic Host for use during the public performance of the liturgy. There is no pictorial or literary evidence for this supposition, however, and indeed their small size would seem to preclude their use for the round leavened loaves standard in both East and West during the early Christian period. From the second century, however, there are references to communion by lay people in private homes as well as to portions of the Host carried from the church for the celebration of communion by those unable or, in the case of hermits, unwilling to attend public services. The fact that the majority of Christian pyxides are devoted to healing scenes suggests that such a use is possible, but the presence of Christian imagery does not preclude secular use, and these small lockable boxes may well have served as containers for valuables.

The two healing scenes to which this pyxis is devoted are placed opposite one another and centred approximately between lock and hinge spaces. To the left of the lock space is *The healing of the paralytic*, from the Synoptic Gospels (Fig. 2); to the right is *The healing of the blind man at the pool of Siloam*, as recorded in the book of

Fig. 1
An early Christian ivory pyxis, sixth century, diameter 5¾in (14.6cm)
London £308,000 ($462,000). 11.XII.86

Fig. 2
The healing of the paralytic

John (Fig. 3). The remaining figures, who are not an integral part of the narrative, function as attendants or witnesses. Such figures, who accompany Christ almost from his entrance into art, have been identified variously as disciples, apostles, evangelists, prophets and angels. On this pyxis, they serve in addition as space fillers, a not uncommon device on pyxides with a limited number of scenes.

The healing of the paralytic depicts the climax of the story, when Jesus exhorts the paralytic to take up his bed and walk (Fig. 2). Christ, who turns towards the paralytic, makes a gesture of speech with his right hand; his left undoubtedly held a cross staff. The paralytic, dressed in a short belted tunic, gazes back at Christ as he walks away, carrying his bed on his back. Two bearded and two unbearded figures flank the scene. On the right, both hold scrolls in their left hands, and the beardless figure makes a gesture of speech with his right (Figs 1 and 2). On the left, the bearded figure raises his right hand in a gesture of acclamation (Figs 2 and 4), the usual gesture of figures who bear witness to the miracles of Christ. Between the heads of the two witnesses on the left and the head of Christ is the suggestion of an architectural setting, perhaps an arcade, but it is not continuous.

This scene finds its closest iconographic parallels within a group of ivories associated with the sixth-century cathedra of Maximianus. The scene does not survive on the cathedra itself, but it appears on the related Etschmiadzin and St Lupicin gospel covers, on a diptych in Cambridge and, in abbreviated form, on a pyxis in Rome. The similar poses of the figures, the presence of the cross staff and of suggested architectural settings distinguish this group. On the plaques the number of witnesses is usually limited to two, who are bearded and carry codices, but as noted above, on several pyxides, as well as on the St Lupicin gospel cover, the number of witnesses is increased to fill an expanded horizontal format.

A model from the Maximianus group can be assumed for the second scene on the pyxis, *The healing of the blind man at Siloam* (Fig. 3). In accordance with the biblical text, Christ reaches out to anoint the eyes of the young blind man who wears a long unbelted tunic and strides towards Christ with his right arm outstretched and his left holding a staff. The scene appears on the cathedra and on related pyxides, where once again the similar poses, cross staff and suggested architectural settings suggest a common model. On this pyxis, however, four witnesses rather than the usual two are once again present. On the right, the head of a beardless figure appears behind the blind youth. Next to him a bearded figure holding a codex raises his right hand in acclamation. On the left, a beardless figure makes a gesture of speech with his right hand; his left perhaps held a scroll. Next to him is a bearded figure who raises his large hand in an unusual gesture that is perhaps also meant to suggest speech (Figs 1 and 3).

This last figure differs significantly in dress as well as in gesture from the other witnesses, although the facial type is identical to the other bearded figures on the pyxis. He wears a tunic with long fitted sleeves and a mantle that falls from his shoulders in a graceful curve across his chest. This form of dress is typical of the sixth century, and can be seen on numerous ivories as well as in the sixth century mosaics of San Vitale at Ravenna, where it is worn by members of Theodora's

Fig. 3
The healing of the blind man at the pool of Siloam

Fig. 4
Witnesses to the miracles of Christ

retinue. There, however, and in every case, this clothing is worn by women; it is in fact distinctively feminine attire. A likely explanation for this anomaly on the pyxis is that the carver, who wished to limit the number of scenes to two, was faced with a model that included an additional scene involving a female figure, whom he proceeded to transform into a male witness by substituting a bearded head of the type found elsewhere on the pyxis. The likelihood of such a scenario is increased when we examine related pyxides from the early Christian period, some of which depict as many as five miracle scenes within the horizontal format. Usually these scenes follow one another without interruption, and frequently scenes are conflated so that Christ is forced to do double duty, participating simultaneously in miracles taking place on either side of him. On these pyxides two scenes are depicted that include women: *Christ meeting the Samaritan woman*, and *The woman with the issue of blood*. In the latter, a woman approaches Christ from behind or stands beside him, touching his garment with one hand, the other raised to indicate her head, the most common source of haemorrhages. On the pyxis the adaptation of such a figure would explain his dress as well as his gesture, which the carver awkwardly altered to imply speech. An arcaded setting is again suggested, but it is not continuous.

Beneath the lockspace is a structure consisting of three columns or piers topped by a triangular form carved with dentils (Fig. 1). Knotted curtains hang between the supports. Although crude in execution, these elements are perhaps meant to suggest a baldachin hung with curtains, an architectural form associated with depictions of altars on pyxides in the Metropolitan and Cleveland Museums, for example. Recarving has obliterated the upper part of similar elements between the hinges making interpretation difficult (Fig. 4).

Stylistically, as well as iconographically, the pyxis belongs to the group of ivories associated with the cathedra of Maximianus. Among the pyxides included in this group are three of high quality, in Florence, Pesaro and Werden, as well as several fragments of lower quality, all assigned to the sixth century. Characteristic of this group is a preference for three-quarter poses and for lively figures who, unless they function as witnesses, relate to one another within a scene. Faces are triangular with small eyes and browlines that curve down and outward at the corner of the eye. Drapery is characterized by thick, heavy folds that, in the finest examples, fall naturally on the body, and in examples of lesser quality tend to form decorative patterns independent of the body beneath. The hems and necklines are frequently decorated with two parallel lines. Backgrounds are indicated by parallel lines suggesting an arcade or by more elaborate, but frequently inaccurately rendered, architectural forms. This pyxis finds parallels on the Pesaro pyxis, where the drapery and faces are similar, and on the Werden pyxis where the figure of a shepherd can be compared to the paralytic. Although there is a continuing debate as to the location of the workshops that produced these works, recent scholarship favours a Constantinopolitan provenance for the cathedra of Maximianus, and the pyxides of high quality associated with it are certainly products of the Christian East, and most likely products of the capital as well.

The Middleham jewel

Richard Camber

The Middleham jewel, named after the castle in North Yorkshire close to where it was excavated in 1985, is one of the most significant discoveries in the field of English medieval goldsmiths' work made this century. It is also, at least insofar as its original function is concerned, one of the most puzzling.

Designed as a pendant, the lozenge-shaped, double-sided jewel has on the front a finely engraved representation of the Trinity, which is matched on the reverse by a similarly engraved representation of the Nativity. Both the style of the engraving and the iconography of these two scenes indicate that the jewel is to be dated to the second half of the fifteenth century and that it was in all probability the work of an English goldsmith drawing on the imagery of contemporary continental woodcuts. Unusually for English work of this period, however, neither scene was intended to be enamelled: instead, they have been burnished in such a way as to create an extraordinary illusion of depth, with the highly polished figures appearing to float against the minute hatching of the background.

Both sides of the jewel are framed by a heavy gold border. The border on the reverse is engraved with the standing figures of fifteen saints, two of whom have been identified as Saint George and Saint Augustine of Canterbury, further pointers, perhaps, to the English origins of the jewel. Much more puzzling, however, is the border on the front: this is surmounted by a large sapphire and is inscribed *Ecce agnus dei qui tollis peccata mundi tetragrammaton ananyzapta*. The *agnus dei* formula occurs in the service of the Mass, which suggests that the jewel may have been intended to hold a communion wafer: it is noteworthy that the Nativity panel on the reverse was originally designed to slide out and that, when removed, it reveals a shallow cavity of the same form as the jewel itself.

Additionally, the presence of the sapphire, a stone described in medieval lapidaries as having a chastening and purifying influence upon the soul, could also be taken as evidence of a sacramental function, since sapphires were frequently associated with ecclesiastics during the middle ages. In contrast to this eucharistic hypothesis, however, due weight must also be given to the presence of the terms *tetragrammaton* (one of the sacred names of God) and, more particularly, *ananyzapta*, both of which

Two views of an English Gothic gold and sapphire pendant, the front inscribed and engraved with
a representation of the Trinity, the reverse engraved with a representation of the Nativity,
second half fifteenth century, height 2½in (6.4cm)
London £1,430,000 ($2,145,000). 11.XII.86

suggest that the jewel may have had a secondary amuletic function. The term
ananyzapta, for example, was regarded in medieval England as a specific charm
against epilepsy or the falling sickness.

Whether the Middleham jewel was designed originally as a sacramental object,
an amulet against epilepsy or a general-purpose talisman, is still a matter for further
research. Although nothing with a known function has survived with which it
may be compared, evidence may yet be forthcoming from a detailed examination
of the contents of the interior cavity, which is now filled with minute fragments of
gold thread embedded in a mixture of earth and roots. Whatever its purpose,
however, the importance of the jewel as one of the few surviving examples of
goldsmiths' work from the period of the Wars of the Roses is unquestionable.

A Netherlandish oak figure of the Virgin of the Annunciation, *circa* 1480, height 43in (109.2cm)
London £16,500 ($24,750). 11.XII.86
The figure is now in the Rijksmuseum, Amsterdam.

Opposite
A pair of English Tudor bronze heraldic beasts, first half sixteenth century, overall height 28½in (72.5cm) and 30⅛in (76.5cm)
London £302,500 ($496,100). 9.VII.87

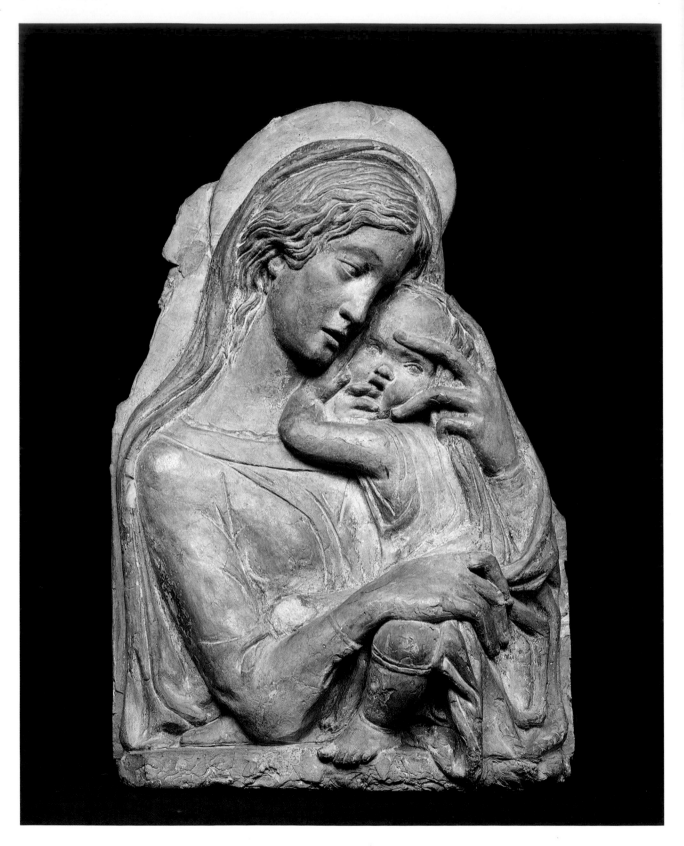

An Italian bronze group of
Hercules killing the dragon
Ladon, attributed to Felice
Palma, *circa* 1614–16,
height 16⅞in (43cm)
London £220,000 ($330,000).
11. XII.86

Opposite
A Florentine terracotta relief of
the Virgin and Child from the
workshop of Donatello,
circa 1447–53,
height 27¾in (70.5cm)
New York $41,800 (£29,231).
25.XI.86

A Florentine *pietra dura* and ebony casket from the Grand Ducal workshop, *circa* 1700–1720,
width 20¾in (52.7cm)
New York $187,000 (£130,769). 25.XI.86
Now in the Minneapolis Institute of Arts.

Opposite
A Venetian bronze allegorical group of Astronomy, attributed to Tiziano Aspetti,
late sixteenth century, height 9in (23cm)
New York $121,000 (£74,233). 30.V.87

A French marble portrait bust of
Anne Audeoud by Jean-Antoine
Houdon, signed and dated *1781*,
height 15⅞in (40.5cm)
Monte Carlo FF3,718,500
(£371,850:$619,750). 22.VI.87

Opposite
A Flemish white marble portrait bust
of François-Henri de Montmorency,
Duke of Luxembourg (1628–95),
attributed to Jan Pieter van
Baurscheit the Elder, *circa* 1695,
height 40in (101.6cm)
London £423,500 ($635,250).
11.XII.86

An English white marble portrait bust of Sir Isaac Ware, by Louis-François Roubiliac, *circa* 1741, height 20⅛in (51cm)

The bust, formerly the property of Sir Thomas Ingleby, Bt, of Ripley Castle, Yorkshire, was sold by private treaty to the Detroit Institute of Arts.

An English painted lead figure of a dog, attributed to John Cheere, *circa* 1760,
height 21in (53.3cm)
London £55,000 ($93,500). 7.IV.87
From the collection of Sir Francis Dashwood, Bt

Nicholas Hilliard
Edward Seymour, Earl of Hertford, signed with monogram and dated *1572*, diameter 1½in (3.8cm)
London £46,200 ($79,926). 8.VI.87

Opposite, below left
Louis-Lié-Périn Salbreux
A young lady, signed, *circa* 1800, diameter 2¾in (7.1cm)
London £20,900 ($31,350). 10.XI.86

Below right
Jean-Baptiste Weyler
A gentleman, signed, *circa* 1785, diameter 2⅞in (7.4cm)
London £18,700 ($28,050). 10.XI.86

Nicolas Lafrensen
The consolations of absence, signed
with initials, *circa* 1780,
diameter $2\frac{3}{8}$in (6cm)
London £17,050 ($25,575).
10.XI.86

Jean-Baptiste Singry
Jeanne-Marguerite-Nicole Lavrillière,
'Mademoiselle Pauline', in the role of
Rosière de Verneuil, signed and dated
1812, $4\frac{7}{8}$in (12.5cm)
London £22,000 ($33,000). 10.XI.86

Jean Petitot
Anne of Austria, circa 1660,
$1\frac{5}{8}$in (4cm)
London £9,240 ($13,860).
10.XI.86

The miniatures illustrated on this page are from the collection of the late Sir Charles Clore.

A gold and mother-of-pearl nècessaire, possibly Augsburg, mid-eighteenth century,
width 4⅜in (11cm)
Geneva SF49,500 (£20,975: $30,183). 13.XI.86

A gold snuff box of cartouche form, maker's mark of Noël Hardivilliers,
Paris, 1732, width 3⅛in (8cm)
Geneva SF60,500 (£24,795: $41,156). 14.V.87

A three colour gold *boîte à surprise*, the interior containing an erotic automaton,
maker's mark of Augustin-André Héguin, Paris, 1784, width 2¾in (7.1cm)
Geneva SF401,500 (£164,549: $273,129). 14.V.87

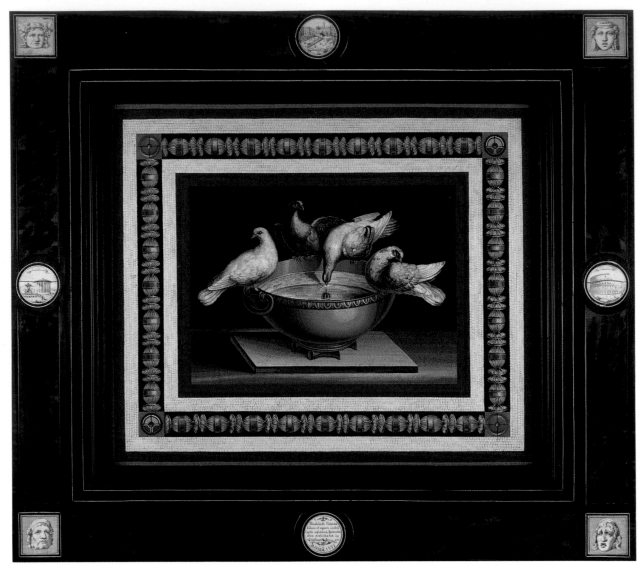

A micro-mosaic panel of the Capitoline doves of Pliny, by Agostino Francescangeli, signed and dated on the reverse, *Rome, 1837*, width 15in (38cm)
Geneva SF31,900 (£13,517: $19,451). 13.XI.86

Opposite
A documentary 'SteinKabinett' by Christian Friedrich Neuber, Dresden, *circa* 1795, width 6⅞in (17.5cm), accompanied by a signed hand-written booklet in French, listing the specimen stones
Geneva SF99,000 (£41,949: $60,366). 13.XI.86

A gold and hardstone snuff box in the manner of F. L. Hoffmann, Dresden, *circa* 1770, width 3⅜in (8.5cm)
Geneva SF275,000 (£112,705: $187,075). 14.V.87

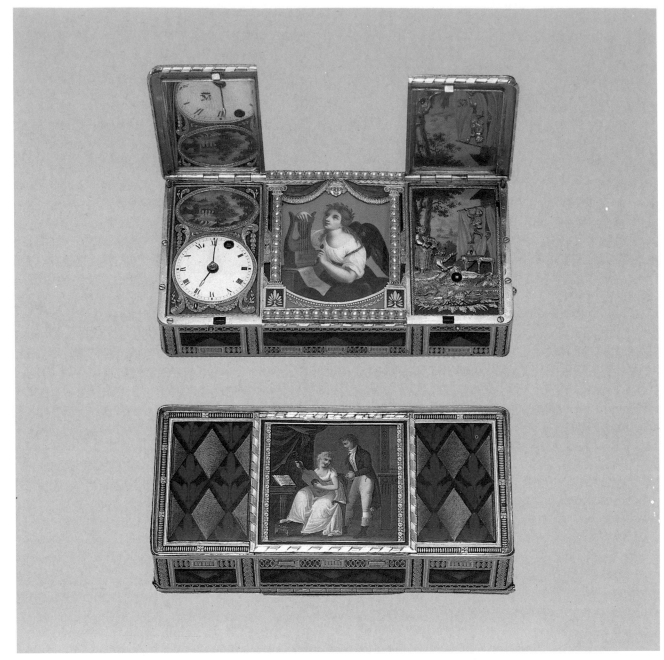

Two views of a two-colour gold, enamel and pearl musical snuff box with watch and automaton,
maker's mark *M* below a coronet, Geneva, *circa* 1800, width 3¾in (9.5cm)
Geneva SF132,000 (£55,932: $80,488). 13.XI.86

From the top row, left to right

A gold and enamel vinaigrette, maker's mark of Gabriel-Raoul Morel, Paris, 1819–38, height 1⅛in (3cm), £3,080 ($5,328)

A gold and pearl vinaigrette, Paris, 1819–38, height 1¾in (4.5cm), £4,840 ($8,373)

A French gold and enamel vinaigrette, late nineteenth century, width 1⅛in (3cm), £1,540 ($2,664)

A three-colour gold vinaigrette, *circa* 1825, width 1⅜in (3.5cm), £1,430 ($2,474)

A French gold and agate oval vinaigrette, *circa* 1800, width 1⅛in (3cm), £572 ($990)

A gold and hardstone cameo vinaigrette, maker's mark of Gabriel-Raoul Morel, Paris, 1819–38, width 1¼in (3.2cm), £935 ($1,618)

A silver-gilt and enamel vinaigrette, maker's mark *TE* in a rectangle, London, 1798, width 1⅜in (3.5cm), £605 ($1,047)

A two-colour gold and enamel vinaigrette, maker's mark of Moulinié, Bautte et Co., Geneva, 1807–15, width 1¼in (3.2cm), £1,980 ($3,425)

The vinaigrettes illustrated on this page are from the collection of the late Eileen Ellenbogen and were sold in London on 18 June 1987.

An Imperial porcelain vase, period of Nicholas I, 1825–55, height 8⅛in(20.5cm)
London £2,860 ($4,319). 17.X.86

Opposite, above
A Fabergé gold, enamel and diamond-mounted carved nephrite easter egg bonbonnière,
workmaster Henrik Wigström, St Petersburg, *circa* 1910, height 2¼in (5.7cm)
New York $41,800 (£25,802). 24.VI.87

Below
A set of six Fabergé two-colour gold and nephrite fruit knives and forks, workmaster Mikhail
Perchin, St Petersburg, late nineteenth century, length of knives 5¾in (14.5cm)
Geneva SF37,400 (£15,328: $25,442). 14.V.87

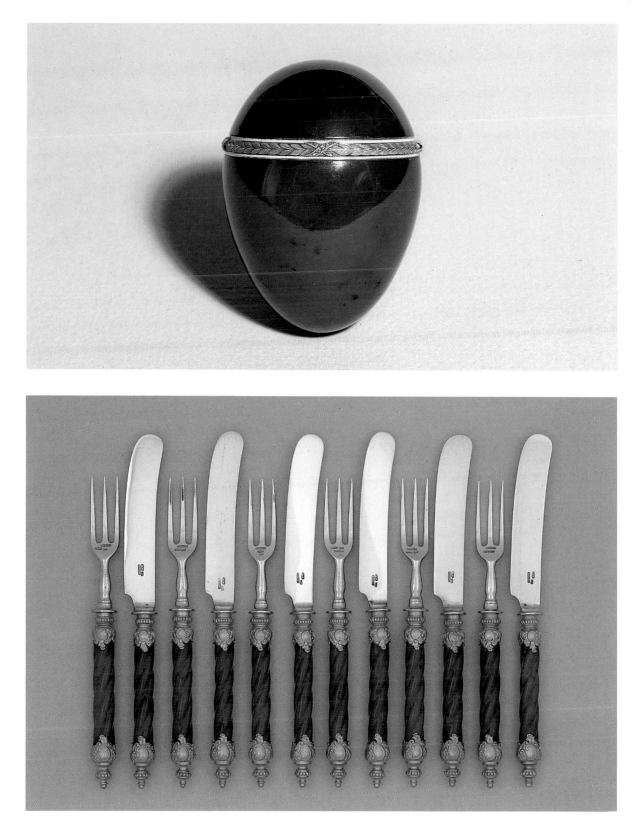

Above, left
A Fabergé four-colour gold and enamel photograph frame, workmaster Mikhail Perchin,
St Petersburg, late nineteenth century, height 5½in (14cm), SF55,000 (£23,305: $33,537)
Centre
A Fabergé gold, enamel and hardstone snuff box, workmaster Henrik Wigström,
St Petersburg, *circa* 1900, length 3½in (8.7cm), SF23,100 (£9,788: $14,085)
Right
A Fabergé two-colour gold, enamel and jewelled cigarette case, workmaster Henrik
Wigström, St Petersburg, 1899–1908, height 3½in (9cm), SF41,800 (£17,712: $25,488)
From the collection of Mrs Leonie Monteiro de Barros

The objects by Fabergé illustrated on this page were sold in Geneva on 13 November 1986.

Opposite, above
A silver-gilt, enamel and jewelled punch set, workmaster Pavel Ovchinnikov, Moscow,
circa 1900, diameter of tray 21½in (54.5cm)
New York $77,000 (£53,846). 12.XII.86
Below
A Fabergé silver and translucent enamel table cigar box, workmaster Karl Gustav
Hjalmar Armfeldt, St Petersburg, *circa* 1910, length 6¾in (17.2cm)
New York $55,000 (£33,951). 24.VI.87

A Cretan triptych showing warrior saints on the outer face of the left panel (here shown closed over the image on the centre panel of the Virgin enthroned) and on the right panel, the apostles Peter, John and Paul, second half fifteenth century, 8⅛in by 16¾in (20.6cm by 42.7cm)
London £50,600 ($89,056). 1.V.87

Although reminiscent of works by Andreas Ritzos, this icon is stylistically similar to a panel sold in June 1981, attributed to Nicholas Tzaphouris.

An icon depicting the Mother of God 'of the Sign', Moscow Court workshop, second half sixteenth century, 12¼in by 10½in (31cm by 26.8cm)
London £2,640 ($3,986). 17.X.86

This is a replica of the miracle-working palladium of the city of Novgorod.

Timeless pieces: watches from the Atwood Collection

George Daniels

The sale of watches from the Atwood collection in Sotheby's New York rooms on 11 December last attracted worldwide interest among collectors, connoisseurs, dealers and those with only a passing interest in horology. With 400 pieces offered for sale it was the largest collection of watches ever to be sold at auction.

Seth G. Atwood started the collection in 1968 with the purchase of a Tompion watch. This was the beginning of nearly twenty years' searching for watches, clocks and scientific instruments concerned with time-keeping throughout the history of civilization. Unlike the majority of modern-day collectors in any field, Atwood made no secret of his desire to acquire the world's finest examples of horological history, art and craft. As a consequence, he soon became universally known in horological circles for his single-minded determination to build a unique collection that would illustrate every aspect of the art of time-keeping.

The collection grew rapidly and soon required a new building especially designed to house it. Within a few years a larger building was needed and this was built at Rockford, Illinois as a luxury museum open to the public and housing some 4,000 examples of clocks, watches and instruments for counting the passing hours. So complete was the collection that where recorded masterpieces no longer existed, Atwood, with total absence of prejudice, commissioned replicas for exhibition. Thus it was that the collection grew into the finest horological exhibition without equal for scope and content.

The news that the Atwood collection was going to be drastically reduced to leave only a small and highly refined nucleus was most unexpected. Much speculation followed on the manner of its disposal, but finally it was agreed that the watches would be dealt with first, and Sotheby's would undertake the responsibility of selling them. As with the Hornby and Belin Collections, sold by Sotheby's in 1979 and 1980, the catalogue was to be a collector's item itself. To this end maximum use of coloured illustrations was made where it was necessary to show the quality and style of the cases and the details of the movements. Experience has shown that such catalogues are much sought after and can reflect the social and economic history of the watches as works of art in an ever expanding market.

Viewing took place during four consecutive days from 6 to 10 December 1986. These were delightful days for horologists for the rooms were thronged with dealers, collectors, enthusiasts and horological students, bent on improving their knowledge. It was a truly international gathering of the initiated, and as great a social occasion

Fig. 1
Breguet No. 2574
A silver and gold cased six-minute tourbillon reverse fusee with chronometer escapement
Paris, 1810–13, diameter 3in (7.7cm)
New York $231,000 (£162,676). 11.XII.86

Fig. 2
Paul Ditisheim No. 10257
A gold hunting cased triple gold bridge one-minute tourbillon with chronometer escapement,
circa 1916, diameter 2⅜in (5.9cm), with original red leather box
New York $170,500 (£120,070). 11.XII.86

as a unique horological event, reminiscent of viewings held twenty or more years ago when sales were attended mainly by impecunious enthusiasts and connoisseurs, whose presence was motivated solely by a love of watches. But general awareness of the qualities of the watch as a work of art has increased dramatically during the intervening period and, as the days passed, the number of serious purchasers viewing for themselves or for clients began to exceed the spectators. By the eve of the sale every important purchaser in the field had been seen in the rooms and there was much speculation about the potential value of the watches.

From the point of view of the investor, the watch has long been a desirable acquisition but the market has been somewhat stagnant during the past few years, due principally to the lack of good watches for sale. The Atwood sale was a remarkable opportunity for collectors to improve their collections and at the same time test the market. Every type of watch was offered, reflecting the four hundred-year-old history of the development of the portable time-keeper, and made by more than two hundred different makers. That the buyers were aware of their opportunities was clearly demonstrated on the day of the sale by keen bidding and good prices. Overall the average price realized virtually equalled the top estimate for the sale, in which the star was historically interesting, the six-minute tourbillon (Fig. 1), sold originally to Sir Thomas Makdougall Brisbane, governor of New South Wales, 1821–25, after whom the Brisbane river was named.

Bidding was particularly brisk for watches with special features. Included in these were repeaters such as the Mudge & Dutton (lot 96), which reflects Mudge's individual style and quality with elegance, and the magnificent clock-watch with alarum and repeater by Sebastian Bauman (lot 82). This form of coaching watch has always been popular, but the hammer price ($24,000: £16,901) was something of a record. Three watches (lots 30, 33 and 34) representing the sun and moon, wandering hour and six-hour dial variations maintained their interest for collectors of the more curious watches, and all exceeded their estimates.

Of the many enamelled watches of all periods, the Swiss nineteenth-century, pearl set watch (lot 180) took the honours for the greatest increase in value, while a beautiful pearl set and enamel musical watch (lot 181) made a very commendable $23,100 (£16,268). A fine astronomical watch by Johann Sayller made $25,300 (£17,817; lot 20), while the solar/sidereal watch by James Green made an astonishing $26,400 (see p. 247). In the English precision watch field Arnold, Earnshaw, Barwise, Cole and Frodsham all sold well and exceeded expectations.

As always, great interest centred on the nineteenth-century Swiss precision and complicated watches. Where these carried a celebrated name such as Leroy & Fils, Breguet and Potter, prices were higher than the top estimates in spite of the petulant view of some buyers that the estimates were too high. The ultimate representative of this class was a one-minute tourbillon by Paul Ditisheim (Fig. 2), always a crowd puller, but this last lot in the sale did not reach the highest price paid. That distinction, as so often is the case, went to the illustrious Breguet with lot 141 (Fig. 1). All in all a very satisfactory day for both seller and buyers and a clear indication that the watch market is looking more buoyant.

Clocks and watches

A Dutch weight-driven pendulum timepiece, signed and inscribed *Jan v. Call*
NEOMAGENS Fecit Chr. Hugenius HAGAE Invenit, and dated *Ao. Dom. 1657*,
height 16⅞in (43cm)
London £121,000 ($182,710). 16.X.86
This clock is now in the Science Museum, London.

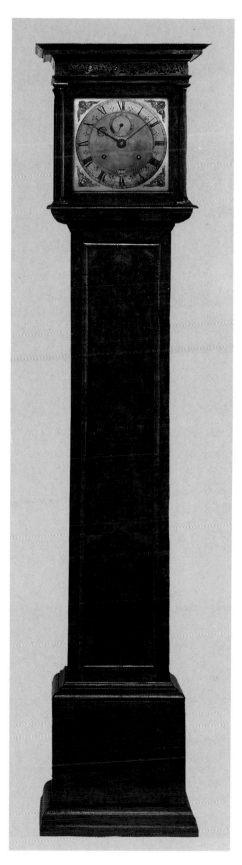

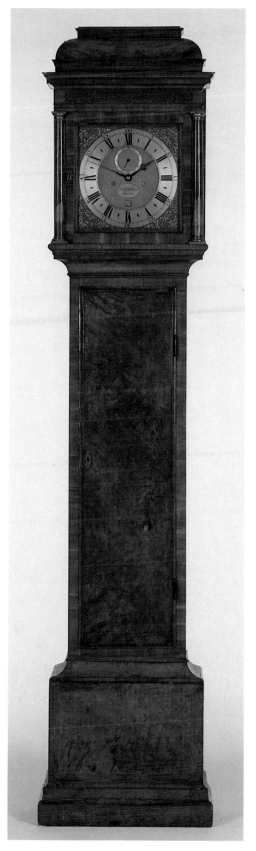

Left
A walnut month longcase
clock, signed *Joseph Knibb
Londini fecit*, *circa* 1675,
height 6ft 7in (201cm)
London £66,000 ($99,660).
16.X.86
From the collection of His
Grace the Duke of Hamilton
and Brandon

Right
**George Graham
No. 699**
A walnut longcase clock,
signed twice *Geo. Graham
London*, *circa* 1730,
height 7ft 5¾in (228cm)
London £28,600 ($42,900).
18.XII.86

Tompion and Banger No. 286
A quarter-repeating bracket clock, signed *Tho. Tompion & Edw. Banger Londini Fecit*,
early eighteenth century, height 11⅝in (29.5cm)
London £79,200 ($119,592). 16.X.86

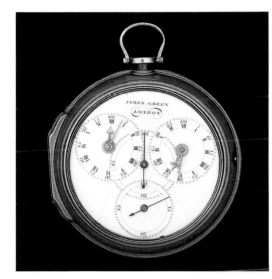

Above

A solar/sidereal watch with epicyclic maintaining power, by James Green, No. 5969, London, 1776, diameter $2\frac{1}{4}$in (5.8cm) New York \$26,400 (£18,592). 11.XII.86. From the collection of Seth G. Atwood

Below

A gold, enamel and diamond pair cased watch by Truitte, Mourier et Compe, Geneva, *circa* 1750, diameter $1\frac{3}{4}$in (4.4cm) New York \$12,650 (£8,908). 11.XII.86. From the collection of Seth G. Atwood

Above

A repousse gold pair cased verge watch by W. Graham, London, *circa* 1725, diameter 2in (5.2cm) London £4,620 (\$6,976). 16.X.86

Above

A silver-gilt oignon watch with enamel balance cock and subsidiary seconds, by Em. Wagner, Berne, *circa* 1710, diameter $2\frac{1}{4}$in (5.8cm) New York \$15,950 (£11,232). 11.XII.86. From the collection of Seth G. Atwood

Below

A gold and enamel minute-repeating hunting cased watch with concealed erotic automaton, *circa* 1890, diameter $2\frac{1}{8}$in (5.2cm) New York \$17,600 (£10,732). 8.VI.87

A gold hunting cased minute-repeating split
second chronograph with perpetual calendar
and moon phases by A. Lange & Sohne,
Glashutte B/. Dresden,
circa 1896, diameter $2\frac{1}{2}$in (6.2cm)
New York $86,900 (£61,631). 29.X.86

Dent No. 32275
A gold openfaced tourbillon minute-repeating
split second chronograph with perpetual
calendar and register, London 1901,
diameter $2\frac{1}{2}$in (6.3cm)
New York $176,000 (£117,333). 7.II.87
From the collection of the Freeman
Family Trust

A gold hunting cased minute-repeating keyless
lever perpetual calendar chronograph
clockwatch with grande and petite sonnerie
and moon phases, diameter $2\frac{1}{4}$in (5.6cm)
Geneva SF46,200 (£19,576: $28,171). 11.XI.86

A pink gold centre seconds wristwatch
by Rolex, *circa* 1945, length $1\frac{5}{8}$in (4cm)
New York $12,650 (£8,972). 29.X.86

Top row, left to right
A platinum and gold tonneau wristwatch by Cartier, *circa* 1918, length 1⅞in (4.6cm)
New York $17,600 (£10,732). 8.VI.87
A pink gold minute-repeating wristwatch by Vacheron & Constantin, *circa* 1942,
diameter 1⅜in (3.5cm)
Geneva SF60,500 (£25,636:$36,890). 11.XI.86
A gold asymmetrical 'Limp' wristwatch by Falcone, Milan, after a design by Salvador Dali,
width 1⅜in (3.5cm)
New York $28,600 (£19,067). 7.II.87

Bottom row, left to right
A gold single button chronograph wristwatch by Vacheron & Constantin, *circa* 1930,
diameter 1⅜in (3.4cm)
New York $16,500 (£11,702). 29.X.86. From the collection of Seth G. Atwood
A gold World Time wristwatch by Patek Philippe, No. 962773, *circa* 1947, diameter 1¼in (3.1cm)
New York $57,200 (£34,878). 8.VI.87
A gold minute-repeating wristwatch by Patek Philippe No. 861492, 1961, diameter 1⅝in (4cm)
Geneva SF132,000 (£55,932:$80,488). 11.XI.86

Judaica

Megillat Esther (Scroll of Esther), an illustrated manuscript on vellum in square German Hebrew
script, eighteenth century
Jerusalem US$30,800 (£18,554). 24.V.87

A Franco-German parcel-gilt silver Torah shield, made by Daniel Hammerer, Strasburg,
circa 1660, height 8in (20.3cm)
New York $34,100 (£23,816). 18.XII.86

Silver

A James I silver-gilt steeple cup
and cover, maker's mark *HB*,
possibly of Henry Babington,
London, 1623,
height 19½in (49.5cm)
London £82,500 ($122,925).
20.XI.86

A George I salver, maker's mark of Francis Nelme, London, 1723, diameter 17in (43.1cm)
London £137,500 ($242,000). 30.IV.86

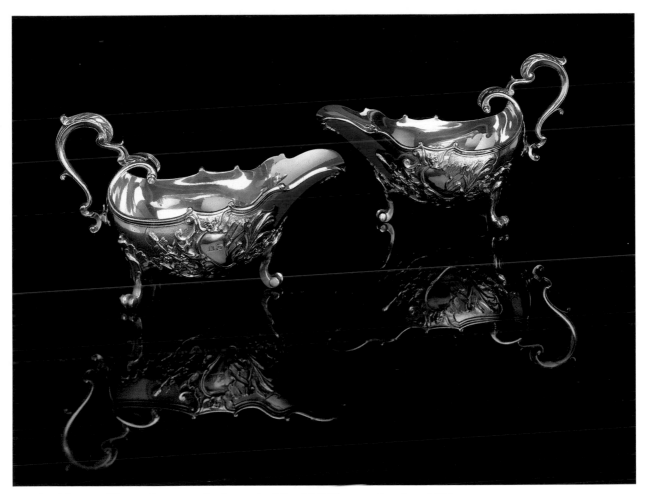

A pair of George II sauceboats, maker's mark of David Willaume, London, 1739,
length 8⅞in (22.5cm)
London £11,550 ($18,365). 5.II.87

Opposite
One of a set of two identical pairs of Georgian silver-gilt table candlesticks after designs by William
Kent, one pair maker's mark of Edward Wakelin, London, 1757, the other pair maker's mark of
John Parker & Edward Wakelin, London, 1775, with four George III silver-gilt three-light
branches, maker's mark of Paul Storr of Storr & Co. for Rundell, Bridge & Rundell, London,
1810, overall height 31in (78.7cm)
New York $110,000 (£77,465). 5.XI.86

A George III 'Jamaica' presentation centrepiece, maker's mark of Philip Cornman for Rundell,
Bridge & Rundell, London, 1803, width 25⅝in (65cm)
London £38,500 ($61,215). 5.II.87

Applied with two identical allegorical panels depicting Jamaica reclining beneath a palm tree, and
armorial bearings of the island of Jamaica and Alexander Lindsay, 6th Earl of Balcarres, Lieutenant
Governor of the island 1794–1801, the recipient of the piece.

Opposite, above
Three silver-gilt tea caddies, two (left and right), maker's mark of Albertus Schurman, London,
1763, the third (centre), maker's mark of Paul Storr for Storr & Co. London, 1821,
heights 6¼in (16cm); 7½in (19cm)
London £10,450 ($15,571). 20.XI.86

Below
A pair of George III silver-gilt salvers, maker's mark of Digby Scott & Benjamin Smith for
Rundell, Bridge & Rundell, London, 1805, diameter 12in (30.5cm)
London £35,200 ($55,968). 5.II.87

An Australian silver and gold inkstand, maker's mark of William Edwards, Melbourne, *circa* 1865,
length 12in (30.5cm)
New York $36,300 (£25,563). 5.XI.86

Opposite
A set of four Georgian silver sauceboats, liners and ladles, maker's mark of Robert Garrard &
Brothers, London, 1819 and 1820, length 9¼in (23.5cm)
New York $220,000 (£135,802). 7.IV.87

The sauceboats are copied from a set of four made by Nicholas Sprimont in 1743–44 for Frederick,
Prince of Wales, now preserved in the Royal Collection at Windsor.

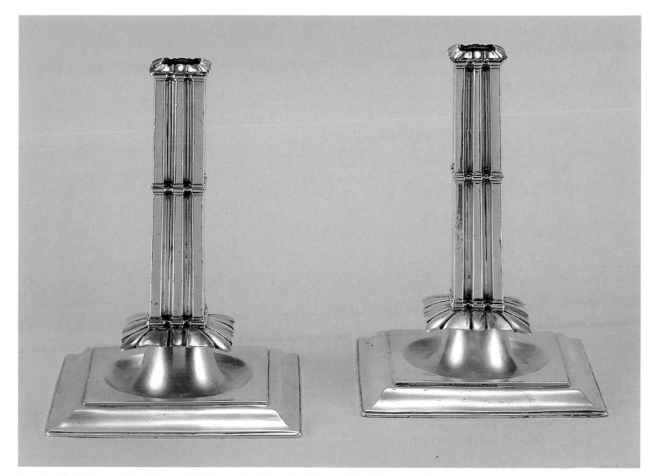

A pair of table candlesticks, maker's mark of Antoine Vassadel, Clermont-Ferrand, *circa* 1687,
height 6¾in (17.3cm)
Geneva SF115,500 (£46,951: $76,490). 12.V.87

Opposite
A parcel-gilt tankard, maker's mark of Evert Kettwyck, Hamburg, *circa* 1635, height 12in (30.5cm)
Geneva SF132,000 (£53,659: $87,417). 12.V.87

Furniture and tapestries

A Louis XIV Boulle marquetry Mazarin bureau, *circa* 1680–90, height 2ft 11in (89cm)
Monte Carlo FF4,995,000 (£499,500: $832,500). 21.VI.87

Opposite
One of two Italian *pietra dura* table tops, second half seventeenth century, mounted on a pair of
mid-nineteenth century giltwood table stands in the style of Louis XIV, width 5ft (153cm)
London £198,000 ($297,000). 12.XII.86

An Italian Baroque marble-inlaid table top, first half seventeenth century, width 4ft 5¼in (135.2cm)
New York $302,500 (£180,060). 16.V.87

A Louis XV gilt-bronze-mounted lacquer bureau plat, attributed to Jacques Dubois,
mid-eighteenth century, width 6ft 3¾in (192.5cm)
New York $583,000 (£413,475). 1.XI.86
From the Patiño collection

Jacques Dubois was received Master in 1742.

One of a pair of Louis XIV gilt-bronze-mounted Boulle marquetry and ebony cabinets,
late seventeenth century, height of each 4ft 2¼in (127.6cm) 4ft 2½in (128.3cm)
New York $797,500 (£565,603). 1.XI.86
From the Patiño collection

Opposite
One of a pair of Italian scagliola table tops, each with an associated lyre-shaped trestle stand,
late seventeenth century, width 4ft 11in (150cm)
London £110,000 ($165,000). 12.XII.86

A gilt-bronze-mounted kingwood parquetry commode, probably Dresden, *circa* 1745,
width 5ft 6⅞in (170cm)
London £231,000 ($346,500). 12.XII.86
From the collection of the late Sir Charles Clore

A pair of Louis XV gilt-bronze three-light chimney-piece appliques, marked with crowned *C*,
circa 1745–49, height 4ft 3¾in (131.5cm)
New York $374,000 (£265,248). 1.XI.86
From the Patiño collection

A Louis XVI Sèvres and gilt-bronze-mounted tulipwood and purplewood *secrétaire*, stamped
M. Carlin, JME, circa 1780, the Sèvres plaques marked on the reverse with interlaced *L*s and date
letters *aa* for 1778, height 3ft 8½in (113cm)
New York $2,090,000 (£1,482,270). 31.X.86

Martin Carlin was received Master in 1766. With two exceptions the porcelain plaques were the
work of Vincent Taillandier who is recorded as working at Sèvres from 1753 to 1790. He probably
devised the '*fond Taillandier*', in which a design of white pastilles encircled by coloured dots was
reserved upon a ground of another colour. This was very much in vogue after 1770. The subtle
mauve-rose treatment of the plaques exemplified here is not known to have been used on any other
pieces of this type.

A Louis XV giltwood armchair, probably by Nicolas Quinibert Foliot, marked with crowned *CR*,
circa 1749
Monte Carlo FF3,663,000 (£366,300: $610,500). 21.VI.87

A German Neo-Classical gilt-bronze-mounted mahogany piano, by David Roentgen & Kinzing, Neuwied sur le Rhin, signed and dated *Anno 1785*, width 5ft 7½in (171.5cm)
New York $209,000 (£124,405). 16.V.87

The title of *Ebéniste mécanicien du Roi et de la Reine* was conferred on Roentgen by Louis XVI and examples of his work were to be found in every European court of importance. The reputation of his Neuwied workshop extended as far as the court of Catherine II, Empress of Russia. This piece was delivered to the Grand Duchess Maria Feodorovna, wife of the future Tsar Paul I, at the Palace of Pavlovsk.

One of a pair of Russian brass-mounted mahogany jardinière tables or buffets, late eighteenth
century, width 4ft 1½in (126cm)
London £66,000 ($99,000). 12.XII.86

A Louis XVI gilt-bronze-mounted mahogany bureau plat, stamped *G. Benneman*, last quarter eighteenth century, width 5ft 4½in (1.64cm)
New York $220,000 (£130,952). 16.V.87

Guillaume Benneman was received Master in 1785.

Opposite
A Savonnerie carpet, *circa* 1810, 22ft 6in by 19ft 9in (685cm by 601cm)
London £60,500 ($97,405). 16.VI.87

A Flemish *feuilles des choux* tapestry panel, Enghien or Grammont, *circa* 1550, 7ft 8in by 12ft (234cm by 366cm) New York $121,000 (£74,233). 30.V.87

Les Bûcherons, a Franco-Flemish pastoral tapestry, probably Tournai, early sixteenth century,
10ft 10¼in by 10ft 2½in (330cm by 310cm)
Monte Carlo FF1,443,000 (£144,300: $240,500). 22.VI.87

Opposite, above
An English floral tapestry arras by William Benood, Lambeth, *circa* 1670,
9ft 1in by 14ft 9½in (277cm by 450cm)
London £33,000 ($58,410). 22.V.87

A settee from a suite of George III giltwood seat furniture attributed to Robert Adam, comprising six armchairs and two settees, *circa* 1765–70, length 6ft (183cm)
New York $220,000 (£132,530). 24.IV.87

Opposite, above
A Regency painted and parcel-gilt settee, early nineteenth century, length 6ft 8in (203cm)
New York $74,250 (£48,849). 24.I.87

Below
One of a pair of George II gilt-bronze-mounted console tables, *circa* 1730, width 5ft 1in (155cm)
Monte Carlo FF1,332,000 (£143,226: $204,923). 30.XI.86
From the collection of the late Countess Mona Bismarck

A George I gilt-gesso side table in the manner of John Belchier, *circa* 1725, width 39in (99cm)
New York $88,000 (£53,012). 24.IV.87

A George II walnut needlepoint-upholstered wing armchair, *circa* 1730
New York $63,250 (£38,102). 24.IV.87

One of a set of ten George III mahogany chairs, *circa* 1760,
London £132,000 ($227,040). 10.VII.87

A George II red walnut library table, *circa* 1740, in the manner of William Vile, width 4ft (122cm)
London £88,000 ($131,120). 14.XI.86

A George IV mahogany breakfront library bookcase, *circa* 1820, width 16ft (488cm)
London £82,500 ($122,925). 14.XI.86

Opposite, above
A George III satinwood, tulipwood and mahogany sideboard, inlaid with ivory, *circa* 1780,
width 5ft 11⅝in (182cm)
London £88,000 ($154,880). 1.V.87

Below
A George III giltwood table, *circa* 1800, with an Italian scagliola table top in the manner of
Lamberto Christiano Gori, late eighteenth century, width 4ft 4¾in (134cm)
London £42,900 ($68,211). 20.II.87

European ceramics
and glass

A Bristol delftware charger, *circa* 1730, diameter 13¼in (33.7cm)
London £28,600 ($48,334). 23.VI.87

A Deruta or Siena maiolica wet drug jar, dated 1501, height 10⅝in (27cm)
London £39,600 ($65,736). 17.III.87

A pair of Kloster Veilsdorf figures of Harlequin and Columbine, modelled by Wenzel Neu, *circa* 1764–65, heights 5⅝in and 6¼in (14.3cm and 15.9cm)
New York $44,000 (£30,986). 9.XII.86

Opposite
A Böttger armorial silver-gilt-mounted coffee pot and cover, probably decorated by Abraham Seuter, with Augsburg silver-gilt mounts, *circa* 1725–30, height 9⅞in (25cm)
London £41,800 ($69,388). 17.III.87

Above, centre
A Sèvres *seau à demi-bouteille* from The Louis XVI Service, marked with interlaced *L*s and date letters *00* for 1792 but made probably in 1791, painted by Charles-Nicolas Dodin and gilded by Pierre-André Le Guay, height 6¾in (17.1cm), $137,500 (£96,831)
Left
A Sèvres *seau à verre* from The Louis XVI Service, marked with interlaced *L*s and date letters *ii* for 1786, painted by Charles-Nicolas Dodin, height 4in (10.2cm), $68,750 (£48,415)
Right
A Sèvres *seau à verre* from The Louis XVI Service, marked with interlaced *L*s, 1791, gilded by Pierre-André Le Guay, height 4¼in (10.8cm), $20,900 (£14,718)

The Louis XVI Service was probably the most famous made at Sèvres in the eighteenth century. It was commissioned by the king in January 1783 and was to consist of 422 pieces, a project that would take twenty-three years to complete, according to a schedule drawn up by the king in his own hand. By January 1793, when Louis XVI went to the guillotine, only about half of the pieces had been made, the majority of which are now in the British Royal Collection.

The porcelain illustrated on this page is from the collection of the late Evelyn Green Davis and was sold in New York on 9 December 1986.

Opposite, above
A Kiel faience table top painted by Abraham Leihamer after an engraving by Johann Esaias Nilson, signed, inscribed and dated *1769*, 21⅛in by 31½in (53.5cm by 80cm)
London £57,200 ($86,372). 7.X.86

Below
A pair of Sèvres pink-ground 'Vases Chapelet' and covers, *circa* 1775, height 13⅛in (33.3cm)
New York $57,750 (£34,375). 16.V.87

A pair of Bow figures of sphinxes, *circa* 1750–55, length 4¾in (12cm)
New York $15,950 (£11,232). 9.XII.86

Left
A Staffordshire saltglaze teapot
and cover, *circa* 1755–60,
height 4½in (11.5cm)
London £18,150 ($30,674).
23.VI.87

Opposite
A Mintons polychrome *pâte-sur-pâte*
vase known as the Solon
masterpiece, decorated by Marc
Louis Solon, signed, 1903,
height 34¼in (87cm)
London £12,650 ($19,102).
21.X.86

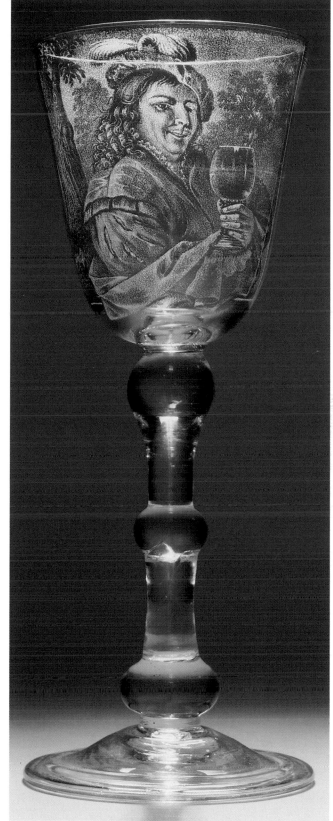

Above
A transparent-enamelled topographical beaker
decorated by Samuel Mohn, signed and dated *1812*,
Dresden or Leipzig, height 3⅞in (10cm)
London £18,700 ($27,863). 24.XI.86

Opposite
A diamond-engraved serving bottle by William Jacobsz
van Heemskerk, signed, inscribed and dated *Ano 1676
in Leyden*, height 9½in (24cm)
London £35,200 ($52,448). 24.XI.86

Right
A Dutch stipple-engraved goblet by Frans Greenwood,
signed and dated *1745*, height 9⅞in (25cm)
London £35,200 ($60,192). 13.VII.87

Musical
instruments

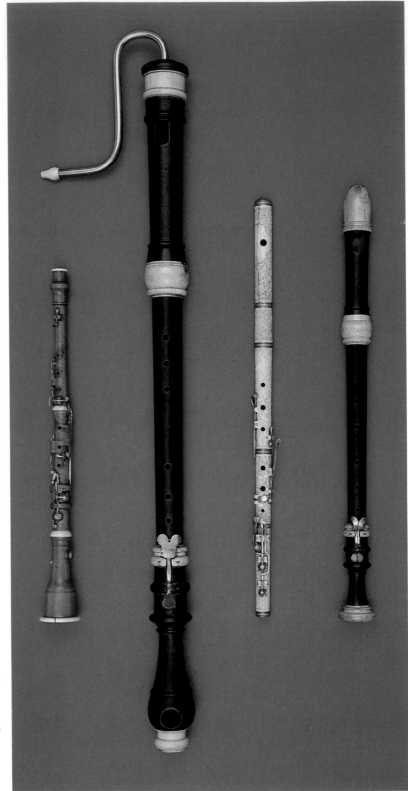

Left to right
A ten-keyed boxwood 'Sellner system'
oboe by Stephan Koch, Vienna,
circa 1825, stamped *S. Koch, Wein*,
length 21⅞in (55.5cm)
London £5,280 ($7,973). 12.XI.86

A stained fruitwood bass recorder by Peter
Bressan, London, stamped *P. I. Bressan*,
first quarter eighteenth century,
length 42½in (107.9cm)
London £31,900 ($48,169). 12.XI.86

An eight-keyed ivory flute by Rudall &
Rose, London, *circa* 1830, stamped *No. 15
Piazza, Covent Garden, London, Rudall & Rose*,
length 23¼in (58.9cm)
London £1,320 ($1,993). 12.XI.86

A stained fruitwood tenor recorder by Peter
Bressan, London, stamped *P. I. Bressan*,
first quarter eighteenth century,
length 27in (68.6cm)
London £24,200 ($36,542). 12.XI.86

A two-manual harpsichord by Jacob Kirckman, London, inscribed *Jacobus Kirckman Londini Fecit 1771*, length 93in (236cm)
London £29,700 ($52,272). 30.IV.87

The 'Nadaud, ex-Kuhlenkampff' violin by Antonio
Stradivari, Cremona, labelled *Antonius Stradiuarius
Cremonensis faciebat Anno 1734*, length of back 14in (35.5cm)
London £396,000 ($696,960). 30.IV.87

The 'ex-Stephens' violin by Antonio Stradivari,
Cremona, labelled *Antonius Stradiuarius Cremonensis
Faciebat Anno 1690*, length of back 14⅜in (36.5cm)
London £154,000 ($271,040). 30.IV.87

A violin by Ferdinando Gagliano, Naples, labelled
Ferdinandus Gagliano Filius Nicolai fecit Neap, 1780,
length of back 14in (35.5cm)
London £35,200 ($61,952). 30.IV.87

A violin by Giovanni Francesco Pressenda, Turin,
labelled *Joannes Franciscus Pressanda q. Raphael fecit
Taurini anno Domini 1829,* length of back 14in (35.5cm)
London £56,100 ($98,736). 30.IV.87

Coins and medals

The French Order of St Michael awarded to Johann Huydecoper, a director of the Dutch East
India Company, in 1650
London £17,600 ($26,400). 6.XI.86
From the collection of J.E. Huydecoper

Johann Huydecoper (1599–1661), a wealthy merchant and prominent figure in the city of
Amsterdam was appointed a director of the Dutch East India Company in 1634. He purchased a
country estate in Utrecht in 1640, giving him the status of 'Lord of the Manor', although he had
previously been ennobled and accorded the title of Jonkheer by Queen Christina of Sweden in
1637. Shortly before his death he travelled to England with a deputation to congratulate Charles II
on his restoration to the throne.

Ancient Greek, Siculo-Punic tetradrachm depicting Dido, Queen of Carthage, *circa* 360 BC
London £29,700 ($49,599). 26.III.87

Ancient Greek, gold stater of Panticapaeum on the Black Sea, *circa* 320 BC
Zurich SF33,000 (£13,983:$20,122). 28.XI.86

Ancient Greek, triple siglos of Cos, *circa* 445 BC
London £16,500 ($27,555). 26.III.87

Roman, aureus of Faustina Junior, wife of Marcus Aurelius, died AD 175
Zurich SF20,900 (£8,856:$12,744). 28.XI.86

Roman, aureus of Augustus, 27 BC–AD 14
Zurich SF39,050 (£16,547: $23,811). 28.XI.86

Roman, aureus of Septimius Severus, AD 193–211
Zurich SF82,500 (£34,958: $50,305). 28.XI.86

Roman, aureus of Elagabalus, AD 218–222
Zurich SF57,200 (£24,237: $34,878). 28.XI.86

Roman, gold bar (211.8gms), second half of the fourth century AD, discovered in Bulgaria in 1904
London £18,700 ($31,229). 26.III.87

England, George III, five-guinea pattern pieces of 1770 and 1777
(both ex Capt. K.J. Douglas-Morris Collection, Sotheby's, 1974)
London £46,200 ($70,224) and £38,500 ($58,520). 2.X.86

Japan, 'Kenjo' oban, Manen (1860–61),
(illustration reduced)
London £17,600 (£29,040). 16.VII.87

United States of America,
Roman finish proof double-
eagle, 1910
New York $38,500
(£22,917). 22.V.87

England, silver penny of King Stephen,
circa 1149, Cambridge mint
London £935 ($1,561). 26.III.87

This previously unrecorded coin provides
new historical insight into the Royalist
campaign in East Anglia during the
Anarchy period.

England, a trial Treasury £1 note of unissued type, *circa* 1916
London £4,070 ($6,186). 2.X.86

The group of medals awarded to Air Marshal Sir Leonard Slatter, KBE, CB, DSC, DFC
London £5,500 ($8,690). 5.III.87

General Cadwalader's wing armchair

Leslie Keno

For the past twenty-five years, the Chippendale 'hairy-paw-foot' furniture made for General John Cadwalader of Philadelphia has fascinated scholars in the field of American decorative arts. The General's position as a military and social leader in the nation's first capital has attracted historians, and the documentation of the interior of his splendid townhouse has been avidly pursued. In *Colonial Grandeur: The House and Furniture of General John Cadwalader* (1964), Nicholas Wainwright, then president of the Historical Society of Pennsylvania, identified and illustrated several pieces of his furniture. The appearance of five 'hairy-paw-foot' side chairs at auction in 1975 and a sixth in 1982 prompted the publication of David Loughlin's *The Case of Major Fanshaw's Chairs* (1976) and the detailed account written by Lita Solis-Cohen for the 1982–83 edition of *Art at Auction,* which ended appropriately, 'The quest for the rest of Cadwalader's furniture continues.'

In 1986, the search was rewarded with the emergence of a Chippendale wing armchair or easy chair (Fig. 1). Unlike the side chairs, which had been discovered in Europe, the wing armchair had been in use in the children's library at the Upland Country Day School in Chester County, Pennsylvania. It had probably descended in the family of Cadwalader's son Thomas to Beatrix Cadwalader Jones Farrand, a noted landscape architect. In January 1987, this chair sold at Sotheby's New York for $2.75 million, the highest price ever paid for a piece of furniture at auction, and more than double the previous record for American furniture. Its reappearance has shed further light on the celebrated suite made for John Cadwalader.

One of the most prominent and wealthiest citizens of Philadelphia during the colonial period, Cadwalader was also a zealous patriot, described by George Washington as 'a military genius of a decisive and independent spirit, properly impressed with the necessity of order and discipline and of sufficient vigor to enforce it'. In September 1768, he married Elizabeth Lloyd of Talbot County, Maryland, and the following year bought a large house on Second Street. Cadwalader was clearly a man out to make an impression. In 1769, his brother, Richard, wrote from London: '. . . Your chariot is at last completed. . . . Were my advise (sic) asked, in a carriage for America, I would have it as light and free from carved work as possible. Such chariots as these are only used from the palace to the House of Lords.'

By 1771, Cadwalader had spent more than £3,600 on the house and employed at least sixty-eight craftsmen to refurbish it. Almost without exception, the General

Fig. 1
The General John Cadwalader Chippendale serpentine-front mahogany 'hairy-paw-foot' wing
armchair by Thomas Affleck, the carving attributed to James Reynolds, Philadelphia, 1770
New York $2,750,000 (£1,785,714). 31.I.87

Fig. 2
A detail of the knee carving showing the peaked acanthus
and cabochon-carved cabriole leg ending in a carved
'hairy-paw' foot.

Fig. 3
The bill of sale dated *Oct 13th 1770* from the
cabinet-maker, Thomas Affleck, to
General John Cadwalader.

Reproduced courtesy of the Pennsylvania
Historical Society.

patronized Philadelphia craftsmen, including Thomas Affleck, Benjamin Randolph,
William Savery, James Reynolds and the firm of Bernard & Jugiez. Each of the
pieces now traced to his house exhibits the sophisticated design and skilful carving
associated with the best Philadelphia cabinet-makers (Fig. 2). In 1774 Silas Deane,
a Connecticut member of the Continental Congress, who visited Cadwalader
wrote, 'I dined yesterday with Mr Cadwallader (sic) whose furniture and house
exceeds anything I have seen in this city or elsewhere.'

Our knowledge of early American furniture is based in part on bills from
cabinet-makers and on inventories. Fortunately, in the case of the Cadwalader
furniture, several inventories and records have survived and were given by a
descendant of the family to the Historical Society of Pennsylvania. The study of
these bills and examination of the known Cadwalader pieces gives ample evidence
of the high degree of sophistication attained in the decorative arts in the late
eighteenth century. The bill from Thomas Affleck, which includes the wing armchair
reads, 'to 2 Mahogany Commode Sofias (sic) for the Recesses, £16, To one large

ditto £10, To an Easy Chair to Sute ditto £4.10.' (Fig. 3). Several other pieces are listed on the bill and the entire charge for carving by the firm of Bernard & Jugiez and James Reynolds was £61. 4.

The whereabouts of the three sofas are unknown, but seven of the original set of twenty 'hairy-paw-foot' side chairs with 'commode', or serpentine-fronts and two 'hairy-paw-foot' 'commode' card tables have survived. The side chairs are now distributed, two in the Kaufman collection, one in the Metropolitan Museum of Art, one at Colonial Williamsburgh, two in private collections and one at the Henry Francis du Pont Winterthur Museum. Both card tables are in the collection of the Philadelphia Museum of Art, together with a portrait by Charles Willson Peale of General Cadwalader, his wife and their daughter, who is shown seated on the card table. The portrait hung in the large front parlour of the Second Street house with five others, including one of the General's brother, Lambert, standing next to one of the 'hairy-paw-foot' side chairs.

Based on the inventories, it seems likely that the wing armchair and sofas were originally placed in the large front parlour with the pair of card tables, possibly two of the five 'hairy-paw-foot' fire screens and ten of the twenty serpentine-front side chairs. For the back parlour, Cadwalader ordered a set of twelve 'hairy-paw-foot' chairs with straight seat rails and a matching pair of straight front card tables. Five of these chairs are known, four at Winterthur and one at Stratford Hall, Virginia.

The wing armchair and three sofas had been upholstered by Plunkett Fleeson by 15 January 1771. According to his bill, they were covered in canvas, while two subsequent bills, one from Fleeson and another from John Webster, detail the fabric and trim used for slipcovers. Blue and yellow silk damask covers were ordered, presumably for use in the cooler months and on formal occasions. For the summer, the General specified 'fine blue cotton check.' All of the upholstery layers were removed from the wing armchair before it was consigned to Sotheby's and a special blue silk cover, which could be easily removed, was made for exhibition purposes. In November, the chair will be placed on loan to Winterthur, where scholars will be able to study it more closely and make recommendations about the upholstery. For preservation purposes, the material will be attached to the frame without tacks, a technique perfected at Winterthur.

The discovery of the Cadwalader wing armchair provides another important example of documented eighteenth-century American furniture, and the fact that it was commissioned *en suite* at such an early date adds greatly to our knowledge of taste and design in the colonies. Now that we know what the matching sofas must have looked like there is hope that these may some day be found. Less than seven years after it was ordered, one sofa was removed by the British who had occupied Cadwalader's house during the Revolution. When General Cadwalader returned in his carriage to inspect his property at the end of hostilities, his agent presented him with an inventory of the contents with the notation 'one settee, Major Knight aid de camp to Genl Howe has borrowed this and not returned. The people at his quarters probably know where it is.'

American furniture and decorative arts

A Chippendale mahogany serpentine-front bombé chest of drawers, Boston, Massachusetts, *circa* 1765, width 36⅛in (91.7cm)
New York $660,000 (£468,085). 25.X.86

A Chippendale mahogany bonnet-top highboy bearing a printed label: *All sorts of Chairs and Joiner's Work Made and sold by William Savery . . .*, Philadelphia, *circa* 1765, height 7ft 10in (239cm)
New York $418,000 (£296,454). 25.X.86

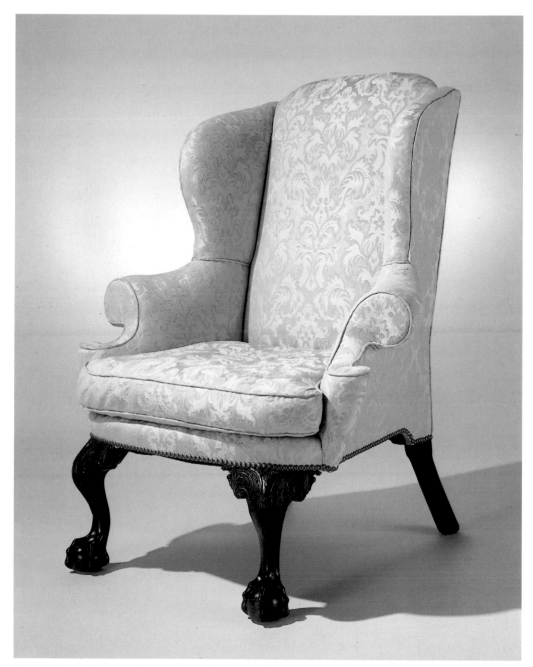

The Willing-Francis-Fisher-Cadwalader family Chippendale mahogany wing armchair,
Philadelphia, *circa* 1770
New York $1,100,000 (£780,142). 25.X.86

Opposite
A pair of silver twenty-light candelabra on torchere stands, maker's mark of Tiffany & Co.,
New York, 1884, height 70¼in (178.5cm)
New York $440,000 (£269,939). 24.VI.87
From the collection of the Kimbell Art Foundation, Fort Worth, Texas

John Carwitham
A SOUTH-WEST VIEW OF THE CITY OF NEW YORK IN NORTH AMERICA
Hand-coloured etching and line engraving on wove paper watermarked
J. Whatman *1794*, final state, sheet size 13⅝in by 19¼in (34.7cm by 48.5cm)
New York $18,150 (£11,786). 28.I.87

A Pilgrim century oak wainscot armchair, Essex County, Massachusetts, *circa* 1675
New York $528,000 (£374,468). 25.X.86

Opposite, above
Currier & Ives
AUTUMN IN NEW ENGLAND: CIDER MAKING
Hand-coloured lithograph with touches of gum arabic, by John Schuller, after the painting by
George Durrie, published by Currier & Ives, 1866, sheet size 18¾in by 28in (47.8cm by 71cm)
New York $14,850 (£9,643). 28.I.87

A needlework sampler of the State House of Providence, Rhode Island, signed *ELIZA WATERMAN's WORK 1788*, and embroidered with a verse, 14in by 12in (35.5cm by 30.5cm) New York $192,500 (£125,000). 31.I.87

A Baltimore album quilt, signed *Sarah Pool* and *Mary J. Pool*, *circa* 1840,
approximately 106in by 107⅜in (269.5cm by 273cm)
New York $176,000 (£116,556). 30.I.87
From the collection of M, Austin and Jill R, Fine

Nineteenth-century decorative arts

A gilt-bronze-mounted lacquer *bureau à gradin* in the manner of Millet, *circa* 1860,
width 5ft 3in (160cm)
London £94,600 ($141,900). 7.XI.86

One of a pair of gilt-bronze-mounted porphyry centre tables in the style of Louis XVI, stamped
A. BEURDELEY, PARIS, circa 1880, width 3ft 4¼in (102.2cm)
New York $159,500 (£108,503). 13.IX.86

One of a pair of gilt-metal-mounted kingwood, marquetry and parquetry library tables by
Holland & Sons, stamped *Holland & Sons* and *Queen Alexandra*, *circa* 1860,
width 4ft 7⅛in (140cm)
London £77,000 ($125,510). 6.III.87

Opposite, above
A Florentine gilt-bronze-mounted marble-topped centre table by A. Barvetti, *circa* 1880,
width 4ft 3⅜in (130cm)
London £34,100 ($60,016). 12.VI.87

Below
A gilt-bronze-mounted mahogany and pearwood marquetry *bureau du roi*, the sides mounted with
oval bisque medallions, *circa* 1880, after the model by Jean-Henri Riesener, 1769 (Louvre, Paris),
width 6ft 2⅜in (189cm)
London £61,600 ($92,400). 7.XI.86
From the collection of the late Charles de Pauw

A bronze group of *Hebe and the eagle of Jupiter* by François Rude, signed and stamped with the
Thiebaut Frères Foundry seal, 1851–55, height 31⅞in (81cm)
London £34,100 ($51,150). 26.XI.86

Opposite
A pair of 'Sèvres' vases and covers painted by Rochette, signed, late nineteenth century,
height 4ft 9¼in (145.5cm)
New York $77,000 (£48,125). 21.III.87

Garden statuary

A pair of sandstone lidded urns, attributed to Jan Pieter van Baurscheit the Elder, first quarter eighteenth century, height 51⅛in (130cm)
Billingshurst £41,800 ($69,388) 27.V.87

A marble fountain, nineteenth century, height 70in (178cm)
Billingshurst £23,100 ($38,346). 27.V.87

Art Nouveau and Art Deco

A gold, cloisonné enamel and jewelled box by Tiffany & Co., 1914, width 5⅝in (14.3cm)
New York $401,500 (£243,333). 12.VI.87

The cover of the box is enamelled after a design by Louis Comfort Tiffany for the Four Seasons
stained glass panel exhibited at the Paris Exposition Universelle in 1900, where Tiffany won a
Grand Prix and five gold medals.

A bronze-mounted, fruitwood marquetry buffet, designed by Emile Gallé, with inlaid mark *Gallé*, *circa* 1900, height 6ft 3⅜in (191.5cm)
Monte Carlo FF466,200 (£50,291: $71,944). 19.X.86

A design for a bedroom by Emile-Jacques Ruhlmann, from an extensive archive of
material from the Ruhlmann atelier, including photographs, documents and designs
for furniture, furnishings and decorative schemes, 1920s
Monte Carlo FF754,800 (£78,299:$125,800). 5.IV.87

Opposite, above
An iron and wood dining table and eleven chairs, designed by Pierre Chareau,
circa 1928, length 7ft 10½in (240cm)
Monte Carlo FF1,221,000 (£131,715:$188,426). 19.X.86

Below
A lacquer table inlaid with crushed eggshell, designed by Jean Dunand, stamped
Jean Dunand Laqueur, circa 1925, the top 2ft 3½in by 2ft 3½in (70cm by 70cm)
Monte Carlo FF854,700 (£88,662:$142,450). 5.IV.87

A stained beechwood and aluminium writing table, designed by Otto Wagner for the
Öesterrichische Postsparkasse, executed by Gebruder Thonet, *circa* 1904–1906,
width 3ft 9⅝in (116cm)
New York $46,750 (£32,692). 11.X.86

Opposite
A bronze and ivory figure of an acrobat entitled *Flame Leaper*, after Johann Philipp Ferdinand
(Fritz) Preiss, *circa* 1930, height 13¾in (35cm)
New York $37,400 (£26,154). 6.XII.86

A pair of oak armchairs designed by C.A. Voysey, *circa* 1903–1904
London £16,500 ($28,380). 4.VI.87

Opposite
A Morris & Co. hand-knotted Hammersmith 'Holland Park' pattern carpet, designed by William
Morris in 1883, woven for 'Clouds', Wiltshire, *circa* 1886–89,
15ft 10in by 13ft 5½in (483cm by 409cm)
London £50,600 ($75,900). 19.XII.86
From the collection of Lord Glenconner

The design and refurbishment of 'Clouds' was commissioned by the Hon. Percy Wyndham from
Philip Webb and Morris & Co., and was carried out between 1881 and 1889.

Jewellery

A diamond necklace, *circa* 1915, $880,000 (£530,121)
An emerald and diamond leaf brooch by Cartier, $715,000 (£430,923)

The jewellery illustrated on this page is from the estate of Flora Whitney Miller and was sold in New York on 27 April 1987.

An emerald-cut emerald and diamond ring, $935,000 (£563,253)
An emerald, natural pearl and diamond necklace, $990,000 (£596,386)

The jewellery illustrated on this page was sold in New York on 27 April 1987.

A diamond ring
New York $2,255,000 (£1,383,436). 15.VI.87

A pear-shaped diamond
New York $1,760,000 (£1,230,769). 21.X.86

A diamond ring by Harry Winston
New York $1,265,000 (£776,074). 15.VI.87

From the top
A marquise-shaped diamond ring, $616,000 (£430,769)
From the estate of Carlotta C. Kirkeby
An emerald-cut sapphire and diamond ring, $924,000 (£646,154)
A ruby pendant–brooch, $1,540,000 (£1,076,923)

The jewellery illustrated on this page was sold in New York on 21 October 1986.

Left
A pair of emerald and diamond pendant earclips by Harry Winston, $962,500 (£579,819)

Right
A pair of sapphire and diamond pendant earclips by Harry Winston, $770,000 (£463,855)

The jewellery illustrated on this page was sold in New York on 27 April 1987.

A diamond necklace–bracelet combination by Harry Winston
New York $687,500 (£421,779). 15.VI.87

A pair of diamond earclips by Harry Winston
New York $137,500 (£84,356). 15.VI.87

Opposite
A diamond necklace by Harry Winston, *circa* 1978
St Moritz SF594,000 (£250,633: $380,769). 21.II.87

An emerald and diamond pendant–brooch by David Webb, $35,200 (£24,615)
A platinum and diamond necklace by David Webb, $162,250 (£113,462)

The jewellery illustrated on this page is from the estate of Pauline Settle Ney and was sold in
New York on 21 October 1986.

An antique emerald and diamond necklace, early nineteenth century
Geneva SF484,000 (£198,361:$329,252). 13.V.87
From the collection of Prince Giovanni de Bourbon-Siciles

The necklace was made for Marie Caroline, wife of Ferdinand I of Naples and the sister of Marie
Antoinette of France. It was later given in payment to Montgolfier, the celebrated balloonist, as
payment for public works in the Kingdom of the Two Sicilies. One hundred years later it returned
to the Bourbon family through the marriage of Prince Gabriel to a descendant of Montgolfier.

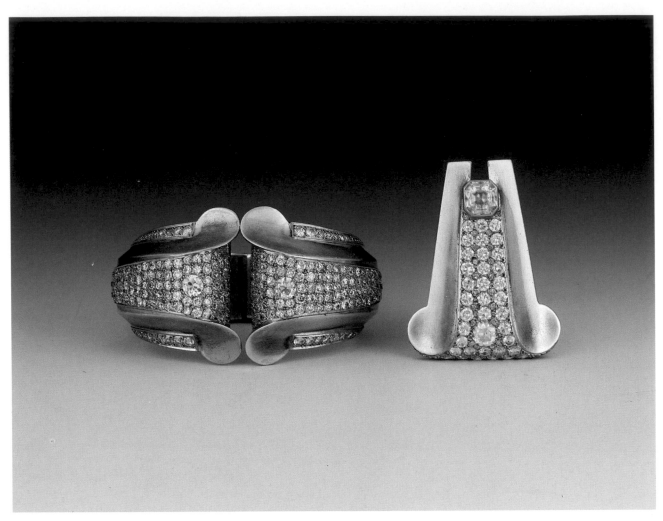

Left
An Art Deco silver, white gold and diamond bracelet by Raymond Templier, 1935
Geneva SF50,600 (£20,738: $34,422). 13.V.87

Right
An Art Deco silver, white gold and diamond brooch by Raymond Templier, 1935
Geneva SF41,800 (£17,131: $28,435). 13.V.87

A diamond, pearl, black onyx and opal pendant–necklace by Cartier, *circa* 1915
New York $96,800 (£67,692). 20.X.86

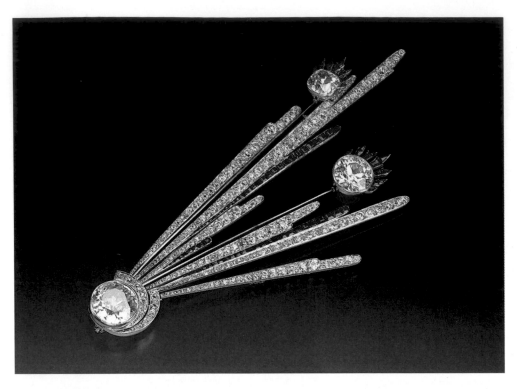

A diamond and ruby
'Comet' brooch,
circa 1910
New York $99,000
(£59,639). 27.IV.87
From the estate of Flora
Whitney Miller

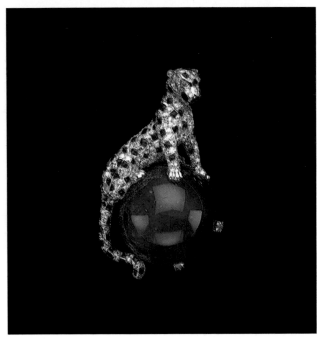

A sapphire and diamond panther clip by Cartier,
Paris 1949
Geneva SF1,540,000 (£633,745: $1,026,667).
2.IV.87
From the estate of the Duchess of Windsor

A pair of invisibly set ruby and diamond
pendant earclips
New York $82,500 (£57,692). 10.XII.86

A cushion-shaped diamond
Geneva SF2,200,000
(£901,639:$1,496,599). 13.V.87

The Widener emerald
New York $539,000 (£376,923).
21.X.86
From the estate of
Ella Widener Wetherill

A pear-shaped diamond pendant
Geneva SF1,100,000
(£450,820:$748,299). 13.V.87

A pair of yellow diamond lapel clips by Harry Winston, 1948
Geneva SF3,410,000 (£1,403,292:$2,273,333). 2.IV.87
From the estate of the Duchess of Windsor

A pair of diamond pendant earrings
St Moritz SF786,500 (£331,857:$504,167). 21.II.87

A pair of fancy colour diamond
and diamond pendant earrings
Geneva SF1,430,000
(£586,066: $972,789). 13.V.87

Above
A sapphire, diamond, emerald and pearl stomacher brooch
Geneva SF407,000 (£169,583: $242,262). 12.XI.86

Opposite
A diamond parure, comprising a necklace with a detachable butterfly;
a lozenge-shaped pendant; a pair of flowerhead pendant earrings;
two butterfly brooches and a cartouche-shaped brooch, *circa* 1860
London £37,400 ($61,336). 9.VII.87

Left
A sapphire and diamond pendant
St Moritz SF572,000 (£241,350: $366,666). 21.II.87

An emerald, amethyst and diamond clip by Cartier, 1955
London £14,300 ($24,024). 19.III.87

A diamond necklace by Cartier, London, 1939
London £82,500 ($138,600). 19.III.87

Opposite, left to right
A diamond and citrine bumble bee brooch, late nineteenth century, £4,180 ($7,482)
A diamond, spinel and demantoid garnet butterfly brooch, late nineteenth century,
£6,380 ($11,420)
A seed pearl, enamel and diamond necklace by Carlo and Arthur Giuliano,
late nineteenth century, £13,750 ($24,613)
A gold, enamel and Roman mosaic brooch by Castellani, inscribed in Greek EUGE ('well!'),
circa 1865, £5,060 ($9,057)
A diamond bumble bee brooch, late nineteenth century, £6,820 ($12,208)

The jewellery illustrated on the facing page was sold in London on 21 May 1987.

A royal client

Nicholas Rayner

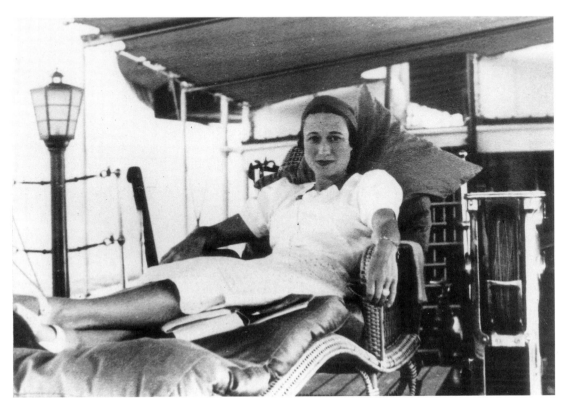

Mrs Simpson aboard the *Nahlin*. Note the bracelet.

The talented jewellery designer has often found himself hampered by the nature of his trade, where commercial considerations all too frequently relegate his artistic innovation to a low priority. The added problem of designing for a specific clientele distracts him from the purer originality which artists in other fields are able to apply. Much, therefore, depends on the attitude of the client, requiring him to forego the traditional in favour of new design.

Few clients could be as supportive of innovation as the Duke and Duchess of Windsor. For thirty years they were prolific buyers in the Rue de la Paix and the Place Vendôme. The Duke celebrated every occasion and every anniversary by offering his Duchess a new jewel and, in addition, the Duchess was wont to buy pieces for herself. At the time of their courtship, the style of jewellery was beginning to change as the geometric patterns characteristic of the Art Deco movement gave way to the more fluid designs of the 1940s. A general desire to escape the gloom and

A diamond bracelet by Cartier, *circa* 1935, supporting nine gem-set Latin crosses, each inscribed and dated between the years 1934–44
Geneva SF572,000 (£235,391: $381,333). 2.IV.87

From the clasp, anti-clockwise, the crosses are inscribed: (1) in sapphire, emerald, ruby and diamond, *Our marriage Cross Wallis 3.VI.37 David;* (2) in aquamarine, *God save the King for Wallis 16.VII.36;* (3) in amethyst, *Appendectomy Cross Wallis 31.VIII.44 David;* (4) in emerald, *X Ray Cross' Wallis – David 10.7.36;* (5) in baguette diamonds, *The Kings (sic) Cross God bless WE 1.3.36;* (6) in ruby, *Wallis – David St Wolfgang 22.9.3(5);* (7) in yellow sapphire, *"Get Well" Cross Wallis Sept. 1944 David;* (8) in sapphire, *Wallis – David 23.6.35;* (9) in platinum, *WE are too (sic) 25-XI-34.*

A wedding photograph by Cecil Beaton of the Duke and Duchess of Windsor in the gardens of the Château de Candé. The Duchess is wearing the contract bracelet.

austerity of the Depression and the Thirties brought about a display of extravagance and style. For the first time, the independent professional woman appeared on the market to encourage a more fashionable and feminine approach to design with which creative jewellers were delighted to comply. With the requirement for spectacular but less costly jewellery, which also coincided with the end of the second world war, the 1940s style came to fruition. Its advancement to full maturity was characterized by its themes of furling drapery, scrolling motifs, random floral patterns, studded with bright sections of diamonds and clusters of coloured stone beads. The Duke and Duchess did not so much introduce the new style as support and lead it as patrons of the most avant-garde designs, not only in jewellery but in other areas of fashion.

Throughout his life, the Duke derived immense pleasure from jewellery and precious objects, possessing an instinctive feeling for design and period. He would

A sapphire and diamond *jarretière* bracelet inscribed *For our Contract 18-V-37*, designed by René-Sim Lacaze for Van Cleef & Arpels, Paris, 1937
Geneva SF1,540,000 (£633,745: $1,026,667). 2.IV.87

The Duchess of Windsor wearing the flamingo brooch, pictured with the Duke aboard the *Southern Cross* in Miami on New Year's Day, 1941. This was their first visit to the United States since their marriage.

have made an excellent connoisseur of eighteenth-century French silver, where so often an unerring and intuitive eye compensates for the lack of authoritative marks. In his quest for quality and originality he rarely patronized smaller artist-designers such as Raymond Templier, although he greatly admired Belperron and later Ventura, both individual and avant-garde designers of their time. He preferred the comforting security and reputation of the big houses, but here he pushed the creativity of their designers further than they would have otherwise gone. With his encouragement and ideas, both Jeanne Toussaint at Cartier and Renée Puissant at Van Cleef & Arpels produced their most subtle and original work, delighted to have a perfect client who not only bought vast quantities of their jewellery but took such an intelligent view of their new designs.

It was fortunate for the Duke that the woman he loved was entirely in tune with his conception of modern design. The Duchess never wore antique jewellery, which

A ruby, sapphire, emerald, citrine and diamond clip designed as a flamingo by Jeanne Toussaint
for Cartier
Geneva SF1,210,000 (£497,942: $806,667). 2.IV.87

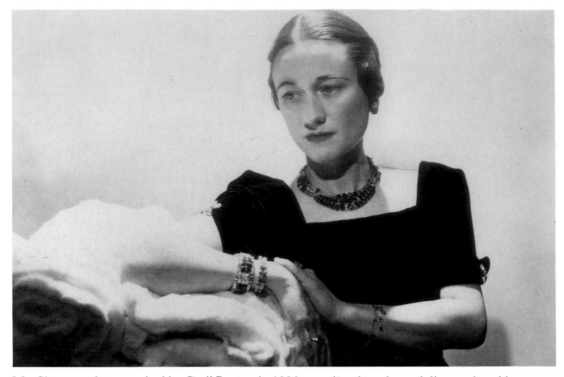

Mrs Simpson photographed by Cecil Beaton in 1936, wearing the ruby and diamond necklace presented to her by Edward VIII on her fortieth birthday. The necklace was redesigned in its present form (see facing page) by René-Sim Lacaze at Van Cleef & Arpels in 1939. The photograph also shows Mrs Simpson wearing the bracelet of Latin crosses (see p.349).

was just as much the fashion then as it is today. Her jewellery had to be so up to date that she had several pieces remounted only a few years after she had first received them. She had a flair for fashion, buying up to three hundred dresses a year, often daring to wear creations straight off the drawing-board and was equally daring with her jewellery. Of small stature, her jewels appeared even more extravagant when she wore them than they seem on these pages. She was able to wear highly colourful creations with elegance and aplomb. Indeed, some of these jewels could have appeared flamboyant if worn without the confidence the Duchess invariably displayed. Many tried to emulate her style but few succeeded.

Rarely do pieces of jewellery succeed as independent artistic entities. There have been many artists who have tried their hand at the craft; Picasso, Braque, Dali to name but three. Each of them treated their designs as extensions of their art and, although they were able to produce miniature sculptures of great merit, none of them succeeded in understanding the relationship that must exist between the jewel and the wearer. The Duke and the designers with whom he worked were successful in establishing such a relationship and in so doing helped to promote a change in style that affected the taste of countless others. Because of the special nature of this art, the client will remain as important as the designer, and the Windsors were the sort of clients of whom every jeweller dreams.

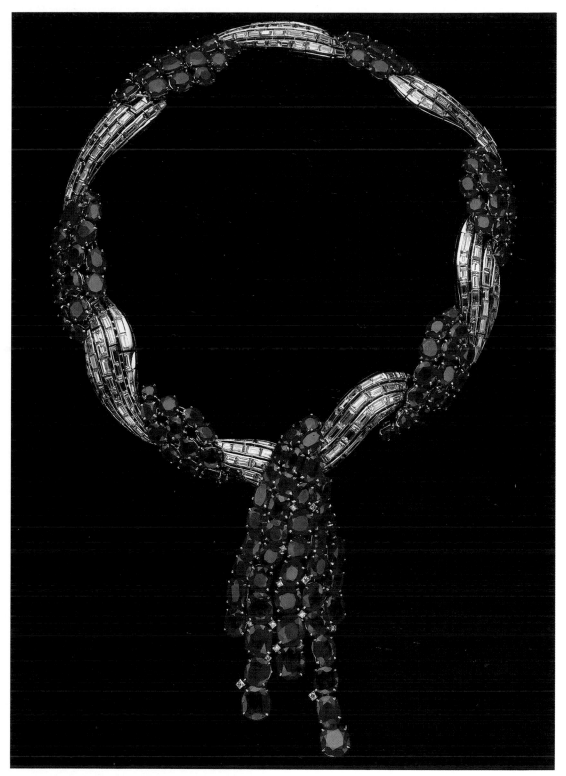

A ruby and diamond necklace, inscribed and dated on one clasp *My Wallis from her David 19.VI.36*,
by Van Cleef & Arpels, 1939
Geneva SF3,905,000 (£1,606,996: $2,603,333). 2.IV.87

Chinese art

Right
A carved stone torso of a bodhisattva,
Tang dynasty, height 37in (94cm)
New York $385,000 (£269,231). 3.XII.86
From the Patiño collection

Opposite, above
A rhinoceros horn bowl, Ming dynasty,
diameter 6¾in (17.3cm)
New York $46,200 (£28,171). 3.VI.87

The bowl is said to have been a gift from
the Merchant Ho Qua to William Couper,
a tea merchant from South Carolina,
active in the 1830s.

Below
An archaic bronze food vessel (*gui*),
late Shang dynasty,
diameter 9½in (24.2cm)
New York $165,000 (£115,385). 3.XII.86

A pottery figure of a horse, late Six dynasties – early Tang dynasty, length 16in (40.7cm)
New York $46,200 (£28,171). 3.VI.87

A glazed pottery figure of a dog, Han dynasty, height 13in (33cm)
New York $63,800 (£38,902). 3.VI.87

A Ming cinnabar lacquer dish, dated 1595, mark and period of Wanli, diameter 13¾in (35cm)
London £24,200 ($42,108). 9.VI.87

Opposite, above
A pair of carved jadeite table screens, Qianlong, height 17¼in (43.7cm)
Hong Kong HK$9,020,000 (£824,497: $1,156,410). 19.XI.86

Below
A pair of jadeite pillows in the form of crawling boys, eighteenth century, length 11⅛in (28.2cm)
Hong Kong HK$3,300,000 (£301,645: $423,077). 18.XI.86
From the T.Y. Chao private and family trust collections

A Yuan moulded blue and white dish, diameter 16¾in (42.5cm)
London £181,500 ($270,435). 9.XII.86

A Ming blue and white dish, Yongle, diameter 30⅛in (76.5cm)
Hong Kong HK$2,420,000 (£186,441: $310,256). 20.V.87

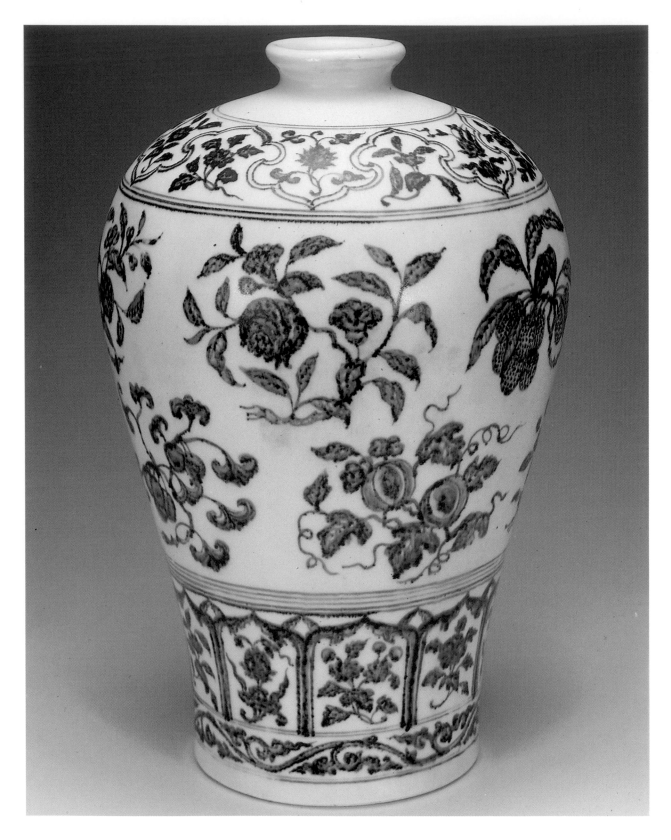

A Ming underglaze-red decorated dish, Hongwu, diameter 18in (45.7cm)
Hong Kong HK$10,340,000 (£945,155: $1,325,641). 18.XI.87
From the T.Y. Chao private and family trust collections

Opposite
A Ming blue and white *meiping*, Yongle, height 14⅜in (36.5cm)
Hong Kong HK$7,700,000 (£703,849: $987,189). 19.XI.86

The T.Y. Chao Collections of Chinese ceramics and jades

Julian Thompson

Mr T.Y. Chao, who formed the collections of Chinese ceramics and jades, sold in two parts in Hong Kong in November 1986 and May 1987, has been for many years a leading and much respected figure among collectors of Chinese art in Hong Kong. With his wife Ya Tsung, whose enthusiasm and eye is no less keen than his own, he had built and refined the collections over more than forty years. His first acquisitions were a spectacular group of carvings in nephrite and jadeite. He then turned to the Imperial porcelain of the Qing dynasty, only later concentrating on the preceding Ming dynasty.

The Qing wares originally included a wide cross section of Imperial patterns, first exhibited at the Chinese University of Hong Kong in 1973. Fine condition was always a prerequisite but few pieces lacking exceptional merit or rarity survived a continuing process of reassessment and elimination. From the early 1970s Mr Chao competed for almost all the finest Ming porcelain to come on the market and succeeded in forming a remarkable group of nearly thirty pieces of early fifteenth-century blue and white. Many of the finest pieces of Ming and Qing porcelain, also of the earlier wares added more recently to the collections, were acquired in the sales of the Edward T. Chow Collection in 1980 and 1981, the only collection to come on the market in the last decade of rival scope and quality.

The two earliest Ming pieces illustrated here both belong to the Ming reign of Hongwu (1368–1398): the dish (see p. 365) and the bottle-shaped vase (see opposite). Difficult to fire, the copper-red pigment painted under the glaze often turned to silvery-grey; both pieces are remarkable for their fine pinkish-red colour. The formal designs of flowers and scroll patterns are also found at this period in cobalt blue, which was used as an underglaze pigment, almost to the exclusion of the more troublesome copper-red, for the rest of the dynasty.

One of the finest pieces of early fifteenth-century blue and white in the collections is the dragon ewer (see p. 371), which probably dates from the following reign of Yongle (1403–1424). No ewers of this shape or design survive in the Imperial collections or, it would appear, elsewhere. The spirited painting seen in the execution of the dragons, the elegance of shape and the contrast of rich purplish-blue with the thick bluish-white glaze, are all characteristic of the best blue and white of the period.

Underglaze-blue is also used in the decoration of the dish (see p. 370, *below*) which bears the reign mark of the emperor Xuande (1426–1435). It is a piece

A Ming copper-red glazed vase, Hongwu, height 12⅜in (31.5cm)
Hong Kong HK$11,220,000 (£864,407: $1,438,462). 19.V.87
From the T.Y. Chao private and family trust collections

made to Imperial order for court use and the blue floral design is contrasted with a yellow overglaze enamel ground, the colour familiar in the Imperial yellow monochromes. Another dish, here seen side view to show the mark written under the lip, is of the same reign and in fact of exactly the same design but with the flowers in iron-brown on a white ground (see p. 370, *above*). The blue and yellow version of the design was repeated in subsequent reigns and the T.Y. Chao collections included rare examples from the reigns of Chenghua (1465–1487) and Jiajing (1522–1566), the last Ming reign in which the design appears.

Although the porcelain of the Qing dynasty (1644–1911) includes many revivals of Ming designs, in a continuing conservative tradition, the three bowls (see facing page), are a startling innovation from the end of the reign of the first great Qing emperor Kangxi (1662–1722). The *famille rose* enamels had just been introduced from Europe and workshops were set up in Peking to exploit the new palette, which included a hitherto unknown pink enamel and an opaque white which could be mixed with other colours. The bowls amply show the delight in the new opportunity for a brocade-like richness of decoration. With the exception of the blue-ground bowls, which bear auspicious inscriptions suitable for the Imperial birthday, the designs are almost never repeated and their dazzling inventiveness at one time led Western scholars to reject the whole group as nineteenth- or twentieth-century fakes. The bowls are also distinguished by bearing four character enamelled (not underglaze-blue) marks which specifically indicate 'for Imperial manufacture'.

The large collection of hardstone carvings included many remarkable pieces in jadeite, the type of jade used for jewellery and prized for its brilliant emerald-green colour and translucency. Both the pair of pillows or arm-rests (see p. 361) and the covered censer (see p. 6), come from the collection of Barbara Hutton. The boys are eighteenth century, the treatment of their faces more sensitive than is found in the much commoner carvings of the last hundred years. The censer is remarkable for the extraordinarily intense emerald-green colour of the stone which has been carved as thinly as possible to enhance its brilliance.

Opposite, above
A yellow-ground *famille rose* bowl, Imperial mark and period of Kangxi, diameter 6¼in (16cm)
Hong Kong HK$1,650,000 (£127,119: $211,538). 19.V.87
From the T.Y. Chao private and family trust collections

Centre
A *famille rose* bowl, Imperial mark and period of Kangxi, diameter 5⅝in (14.2cm)
Hong Kong HK$1,980,000 (£180,987: $253,846). 18.XI.86
From the T.Y. Chao private and family trust collections

Below
One of a pair of blue-ground *famille rose* bowls, Imperial mark and period of Kangxi,
diameter 5¾in (14.6cm)
Hong Kong HK$2,310,000 (£177,966; $296,154). 19.V.87
From the T.Y. Chao private and family trust collections

A Ming underglaze-brown decorated dish, mark and period of Xuande, diameter 11¾in (29.8cm)
Hong Kong HK$3,300,000 (£254,237: $423,077). 19.V.87
From the T.Y. Chao private and family trust collections

A Ming blue and white ewer, Yongle, height 8⅞in (22.5cm)
Hong Kong HK$5,720,000 (£440,678: $733,333). 19.V.87
From the T.Y. Chao private and family trust collections

Opposite
A Ming yellow-ground dish, mark and period of Xuande, diameter 11⅞in (30.1cm)
Hong Kong HK$3,300,000 (£301,645: $423,077). 18.XI.86
From the T.Y. Chao private and family trust collections

An export *famille rose* dish, decorated after Francesco Albani, early Qianlong,
diameter 15⅛in (38.4cm)
Monte Carlo FF244,200 (£24,692: $40,231). 22.VI.87
From the collection of François Hervouët

An export *Compagnie-des-Indes* tureen and cover in the form of a figure of Budai, Yongzheng–early
Qianlong, height 14¼in (36.2cm)
Monte Carlo FF943,500 (£95,399:$155,437). 22.VI.87

An export armorial basin, *circa* 1743, diameter 15⅝in (39.7cm)
New York $99,000 (£64,286). 29.I.87

Opposite, above
An export *famille rose* oval basin from a design by Cornelis Pronk, *circa* 1740,
diameter 18¾in (47.6cm)
New York $74,250 (£48,214). 29.I.87

Below
An export topographical punch bowl, enamelled with a view of Copenhagen, Qianlong,
diameter 15¾in (40cm)
Monte Carlo FF396,000 (£40,040: $65,239). 22.VI.87
From the collection of François Hervouët

Above
Anonymous
A MYRIAD VALLEYS
Handscroll, ink and light colour
on silk, with seventeen collectors'
seals on the painting,
thirteenth–fifteenth century,
formerly attributed to Juran,
active *circa* 960–985,
16¾in by 96¾in
(42.5cm by 245.7cm)
New York $209,000 (£126,667).
2.VI.87

Attributed to Ma Yuan
ALBUM OF LANDSCAPES
One of ten leaves in an album, ink and colour on silk, early thirteenth century,
10½in by 10¾in (26.6cm by 27.3cm)
New York $319,000 (£223,077). 4.XII.86

Attributed to Zhang Wu
THE EIGHT IMMORTALS OF THE WINE CUP, AFTER ZHAO MENGFU
Detail of a handscroll, ink on paper, signed, titled, inscribed by and with the seal of the artist
Zhang Wu, and dated 1363, 12⅞in by 141in (32.8cm by 357.3cm)
New York $88,000 (£61,539). 4.XII.86

Wu Hufan

LANDSCAPE

Ink on paper, signed, inscribed and dated 1954, seventh month, with two seals of the artist and
one collector's seal, 30¾in by 52in (78cm by 132cm)
Hong Kong HK$440,000 (£33,898: $56,410). 21.V.87

Zhang Daqian
THE LAND OF IMMORTALS
Ink and colour on paper, signed,
inscribed and dated 1982, with four
seals of the artist and one collector's
seal, 83in by 36⅝in (211cm by 93cm)
Hong Kong HK$1,870,000
(£144,068:$239,744). 21.V.87

An inside-painted glass portrait snuff bottle by Ye Zhongsan the Elder, signed and dated middle autumn, 1908
New York $40,700 (£28,865).
27.X.86
From the collection of
Janos Szekeres

An Imperial carved Peking glass snuff bottle, eighteenth century
New York $26,400 (£16,196).
5.VI.87
From the collection of
Janos Szekeres

A jadeite snuff bottle, 1750–1850
New York $13,200 (£8,098).
5.VI.87
From the collection of
Janos Szekeres

An Imperial carved ivory snuff bottle, mark and period of Qianlong
London £38,500 ($67,375).
28.IV.87

A chalcedony snuff bottle, inscribed Xingyouheng tang, 1810–54
London £8,250 ($13,448).
3.III.87
From the collection of the late
Eric Young

An enamelled porcelain snuff bottle, mark and period of Qianlong
London £29,700 ($48,411).
3.III.87
From the collection of the late
Eric Young

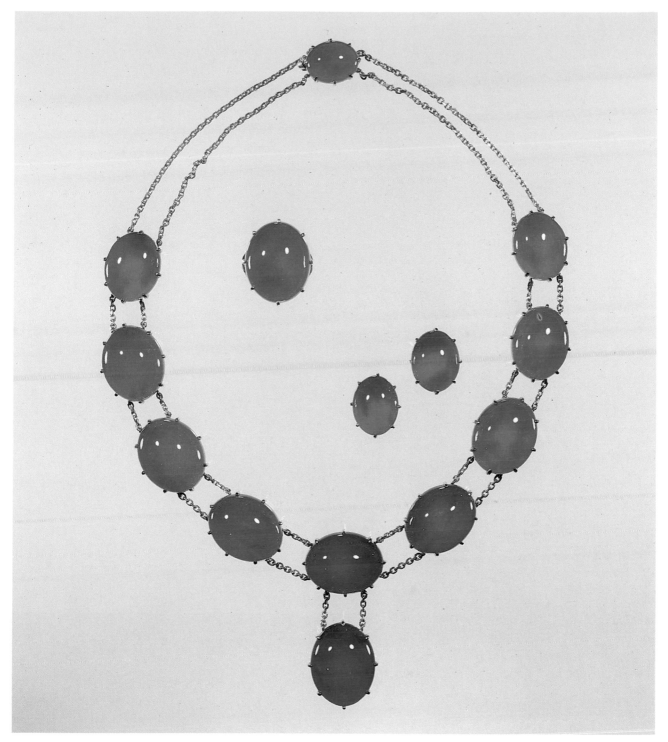

A suite of jadeite jewellery comprising a necklace, a pair of earrings and a ring
Hong Kong HK$8,140,000 (£744,059: $1,043,590). 19.XI.86

Japanese art

A wood figure of Amida Nyorai, Heian period (800–1185), height 55⅛in (140cm)
Amsterdam Dfl 195,500 (£61,094: $87,668). 17.XII.86

Left
An ivory *netsuke* of a *baku* by Gechu, signed, late eighteenth century
London £110,000 ($189,200). 17.VI.87

Right
An ivory *netsuke* of a deer by Okatomo, signed, late eighteenth century
London £44,000 ($75,680). 17.VI.87

Below, left
A five case *inro* with a bamboo *netsuke* in the form of a chestnut by Shibata Zeshin, signed, nineteenth century
London £25,300 ($37,950). 13.XI.86

Below
A four case *inro* by Nomura Katsumori, signed, late nineteenth century
London £12,650 ($20,873). 13.III.87

Utamaro
SHIOHI NO TSUTO (GIFTS OF THE EBB-TIDE)
The first edition of a folding album, 10¼in by 7⅜in (25.9cm by 18.7cm)
London £41,800 ($62,700). 18.XII.86

A Kakiemon-style model of a *shishi*, late seventeenth century, height 10⅜in (26.3cm)
London £48,400 ($79,860). 13.III.87

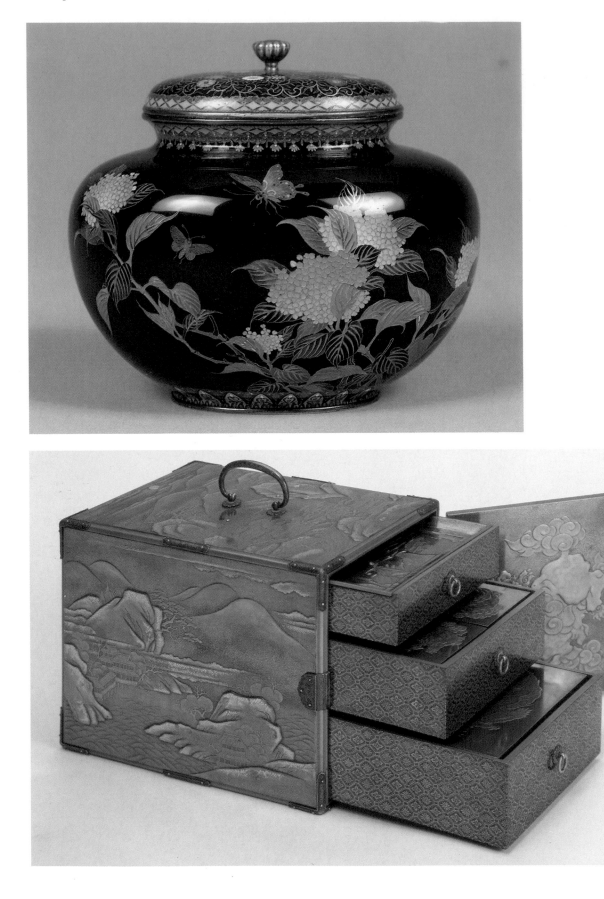

A pair of earthenware vases by Yabu Meizan, signed, Meiji period (1868–1912),
height 9½in (24.2cm)
New York $24,200 (£14,847). 4.VI.87

Opposite, above
A cloisonné jar and cover by Hayashi Kodenji, signed, Meiji period,
height 3⅞in (10cm)
London £9,350 ($15,428). 13.III.87

Below
A gold lacquer *kodansu*, nineteenth century, width 6¾in (17.1cm)
London £27,500 ($41,250). 13.XI.86

A Neolithic Greek goddess

Saul S. Weinberg

Greek Neolithic figurines, in any form or material, have never played a stellar role in auctions around the world. In fact, I am not aware that any was ever auctioned before the New York sale at Sotheby's of a majestic figure, tentatively identified as a goddess (Fig. 1). This was indeed a supernova in the field of archaeological artifacts, a phenomenon which, in this case, is not too difficult to explain.

Marble, or stone, figurines of the Neolithic period in the Aegean area are comparatively rare, and are likely to remain so. Of the anthropomorphic images, in which the human form is developed fully in three dimensions, we know of only forty-two; there are many more of the abstract types, often called 'slab' figures. Within the former group there is an even rarer class of seated females, such as the one sold in the past year; only seven of these are known. There are, as well, some similar seated figures in clay, which are contemporary with, or in some cases pre-date, the stone statuettes.

It is clear from both the clay and stone examples which come from controlled excavations, that the clay group appears with the first Neolithic inhabitants of Greece, as early as 6000 BC, if not somewhat earlier. The stone figures are less well documented, for only three stone images came from a reliable context. Together, they indicate that stone figurines seem to have been made no earlier than the late Middle Neolithic period, *circa* 5000 BC, and continued to be made into the early fourth millennium. Each series, in both clay and stone, begins with the most realistic types and degenerates to more abstract and less carefully made examples. Certainly, the piece under discussion is among the finest in the group of three-dimensional anthropomorphic figures, and there is only one of comparable quality among the smaller number of seated images. The latter was found long ago and is now in Brussels, in the Musée du Cinquantenaire. Its supposed provenance, from the island of Amorgos in the Cyclades, is so tenuous that it has been omitted in the most recent catalogues, where it is listed rather as 'provenance unknown'. That is equally true of the present figure and of most of the forty-two stone figurines. Only one of the seated females has a somewhat reliable find-spot at Sangri on the island of Naxos, but even there it was a chance find.

Without giving too much credence to the stated provenance of all of the stone figures, one can perhaps get some idea of the centres of production by making a geographical analysis: eight are said to be from Thessaly, ten from Attica, Aigina and the Megarid, eight from the Peloponnesos, four from the Cyclades, five from

Fig. 1
An Attic marble figurine, late Middle Neolithic period, *circa* 5000 BC, height 8in (20.3cm)
New York $1,320,000 (£929,577). 24.XI.86
From the collection of the late James Johnson Sweeney

Fig. 2
A view of the figurine showing the
contrast between the enormous
buttocks and legs, and the
slab-like upper body and arms

Crete and seven of unknown provenance. By far the majority came from mainland
Greece, most particularly from the central region. One of the most recently found
seated figures is part of a grave group found in Attica where a similar figure, of
lesser quality, is also said to have been found, at Patissia. The most probable place
of origin of the Sotheby's piece is Attica, but this is only an educated guess.

The Neolithic figures, both clay and stone, share certain physical characteristics.
In most, there is a drastic contrast between upper and lower body. Below the waist
the figures are steatopygous (fat-buttocked), while above they are much thinner,
almost slab-like (Fig. 2). Such limited obesity is known in nature, especially in
parts of Africa, where Hottentot women best display this physical phenomenon.
Stylistically the goddess is related to the earliest Cycladic figurines, even though
they are separated by more than a millennium. Like the Neolithic group, those
made later in the Cyclades have both an anthropomorphic and an abstract type;
the so-called 'fiddle' figurines. In both of the Cycladic types, some steatopygy
remains in the earliest examples, and the angular treatment of the torso continues,
carrying on a tradition most clearly exemplified in the splendid figure of an earlier
period sold at Sotheby's.

Antiquities and Asian art

A Roman marble sarcophagus, second quarter third century AD, width 84in (213.4cm)
New York $275,000 (£168,712). 29.V.87
From the collection of the late Flora Whitney Miller

An Egyptian bronze group of Isis and
Horus, Saite Period, *circa* 664–525 BC,
height 16½in (42cm)
London £20,350 ($30,525). 8.XII.86

Opposite
An Egyptian diorite head of the
goddess Sekhmet from the Temple
of Mut at Karnak, Thebes,
Eighteenth Dynasty, reign of
Amenhotep III (1403–1365 BC),
height 10½in (26.7cm)
New York $55,000 (£38,732).
24.XI.86
From the collection of Lee Radziwill

A Paestan pottery Lebes Gamikos and
cover by the painter of Naples 2585, fourth
century BC, height 22in (55.9cm)
London £55,000 ($89,650). 13.VII.87

Opposite
An Attic black-figure pottery neck
amphora from the circle of the Antimenes
painter, *circa* 520–510 BC,
height 18½in(47cm)
London £44,000 ($72,160). 14.VII.87

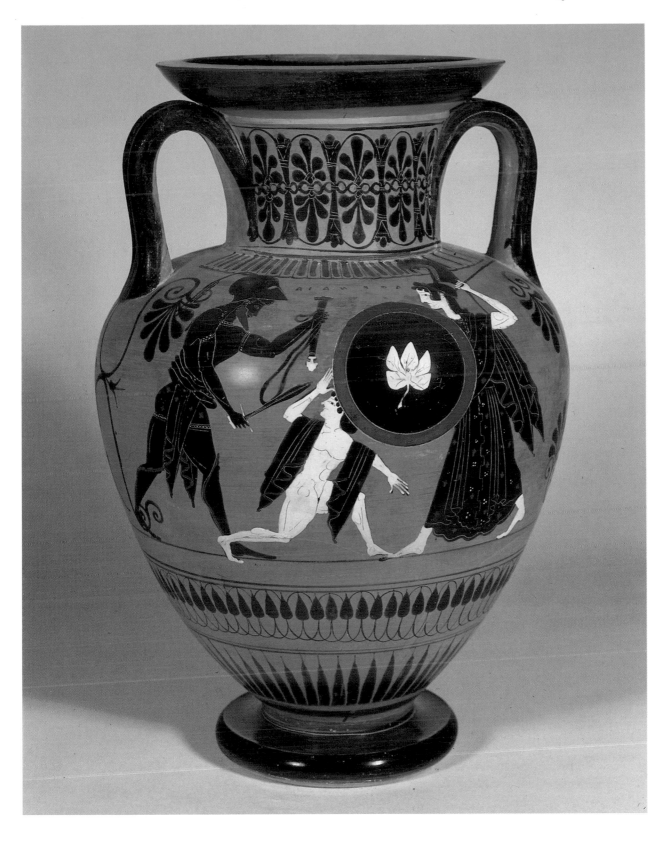

A Greek bronze helmet of Corinthian type, late sixth century BC, length 11in (27.9cm)
New York $71,500 (£43,865). 29.V.87

Opposite
An Assyrian gypsum relief fragment from the northwest palace of Ashurnasirpal II at Nimrud,
885–856 BC, 26¾in by 22½in (68cm by 57.1cm)
New York $451,000 (£317,606). 24.XI.86
From the collection of Rockford College

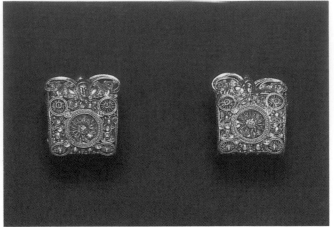

A pair of Etruscan gold earrings, second half
sixth century BC
London £14,200 ($23,146). 13.VII.87

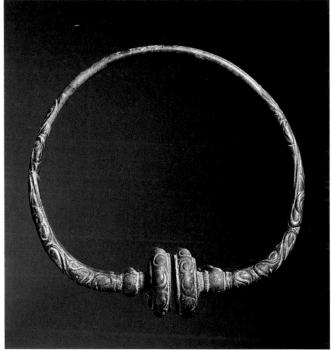

Above
A Celtic bronze torque, Saarland, West Germany,
circa third–second century BC
London £24,200 ($39,446). 13.VII.87

Left
An Umbro–Etruscan bronze figure of a priest,
circa fourth century BC, height 12in (30.5cm)
London £29,700 ($44,550). 8.XII.86

A Sino–Tibetan gilt-bronze figure of
Aryavalokitesvara, eighteenth century,
height 39⅜in (100cm)
London £11,000 ($19,140). 15.VI.87

A Khmer sandstone antefix depicting a Dvarapala, Banteai Srei style, tenth century,
height 21⅝in (55cm)
London £26,400 ($39,336). 24.XI.86
From the collection of M. Norbert Guyot de la Pommeraye

Opposite
A South Indian bronze figure of Siva Nataraja, Chola, twelfth–thirteenth century,
height 30¾in (78cm)
London £145,200 ($216,348). 24.XI.86

Messenger of the gods: a Benin bronze figure

Philip J.C. Dark

The fine bronze figure sold at Sotheby's in November 1986 is one of at least sixteen examples of the representation in the round, in a surprisingly large form of casting, of a type of Benin figure usually referred to as a 'messenger' (see opposite). In general the figures appear similar, differing only in detail. They are characterized by the same type of hat, the cross on the chest, a blacksmith's hammer in the left hand, some form of tie of the kilt on the left hip, the right thumb is generally raised and they have 'cat's whiskers' or vibrissae at each corner of the mouth.

The Sotheby's messenger figure is a splendid example of the skill of the Benin bronze casters' art and manifests clearly a precision of execution in modelling low relief forms and of chasing details. It would seem to form a 'pair', a not infrequent feature of Benin art, with one in the University Museum, Philadelphia. They have certain features in common, notably the same form of cross worn on the chest, though the present figure is, I think, unique in having crosses bordering the two large tassels at the hip and decorating the centre piece of each. Further, the three coils of his belt are similarly decorated. Comparable crosses, suggestive of the Maltese cross, occur on messenger figures in the British Museum and in the Nigerian National Museums. However, crosses represented on other messenger figures vary, and one should, therefore, be cautious in referring to the crosses as 'Maltese', or in considering that they had a Christian origin, via the Portuguese.

The messenger's kilt attracts attention by the variety of its chased forms, which include elaborate guilloches, quatrefoils and a leaf as space fillers between different depictions of heads (the Bini artist has a *horror vacui*). There are three frontal views of what we can assume to be Europeans, which surely caricature a Portuguese with his floppy moustache and bedraggled goatee (somewhat unkempt because of Benin's humidity?). The front view of an African head can also be seen, as well as two abstract representations of Portuguese heads (bottom row, front and back). Further, in each row at the back are three profile views, again of Portuguese; one is shown with an arm and a hand not quite tweaking his nose. The representation of Portuguese in a similar manner persisted in Benin art from the earliest examples of the sixteenth century to the present.

There are other representations in Benin art of this messenger figure. Two shield-shaped plaques, one which used to be in the Pitt Rivers Museum at Farnham, the other in the British Museum, form a pair, each depicting two

A Benin bronze figure of a messenger, Nigeria, late seventeenth–early eighteenth century, height 24⅝in (62.5cm)
New York $792,000 (£557,746). 18.XI.86

messengers holding long staffs in their right hands and wearing coral bead chokers. Several figures broken from stands, varying in size from fifteen to twenty centimetres, which were undoubtedly part of some large altarpiece, are close in style to the large messenger figures, although they had long staffs similar to those on the shield plaques mentioned above. All the aforementioned have vibrissae, but there are other similar small messenger figures from stands, which lack vibrissae but share other features. To this complex of whiskered forms one should perhaps add the superb early head in the Nigerian National Museums collections, which depicts four rather than three vibrissae from each corner of the mouth, and the two diminutive similarly be-whiskered heads in the British Museum. There are also twelve or more Benin castings of bronze horsemen in various collections, of which four have whiskers at the corners of the mouth.

Various interpretations of these so-called messenger figures have been offered. One explanation advanced by Frank Willet, identifying the cross on the chest, the distinctive hat and the staff as symbols sent by the Oni (king) of Ife to Benin in recognition of an Oba's (king's) accession, suggests that they were, therefore, depictions of the Oni's messengers. But only the figures on the two shield plaques and those broken from stands carried staffs in their right hands; the tall messenger figures held only a blacksmith's hammer, the symbol of Ogun, the god of iron, in their left hands. Vibrissae are represented on early Ife terracotta heads but such scarification marks are not used today by the Yoruba. They do, however, seem to be a mark of people now living in the Niger-Benue river area, such as the Nupe, as Joseph Nevadomsky has pointed out in *African Arts* (1986). Further, in Benin itself, such marks are recognized specifically as Nupe, or in general parlance, as non-Bini. It is tempting to accept Nevadomsky's plausible arguments for identifying the Benin bronze horseman he is concerned with as representing the Ata (king) of Idah, which was situated to the north-east of Benin on the Niger river and, by extension, associating other whiskered works of art with that monarch. Perhaps the be-whiskered early head in the Nigerian National Museums collections, referred to above, was a commemorative bronze trophy of the Ata of Idah.

But what of the two small heads from the British Museum? And of the complex of small be-whiskered messengers that seem to have formed part of an altarpiece? Paula Ben-Amos writes that the messenger figures are considered by the Bini to be representations of the priest of Osanobua, the creator god and supreme deity of the Edo. There were, and perhaps still are, three shrines in Benin city to Osanobua which are said to be on the sites of churches built by the Portuguese in the sixteenth century. Their guardian, Ohesa, is reported to have worn a cross. Were then the large messenger figures, like the one sold at Sotheby's, originally cast as furniture for such shrines, and the smaller ones incorporated into the bronze altars placed on them? The cross would associate the figures with Osanobua and the whiskers and blacksmith's hammer with Ogun, god of warriors, and the victory of the Edo over the Ata of Idah in Oba Esigie's reign in the sixteenth century, thus expressing the spiritual and temporal powers that pertain in Benin.

Tribal art

A Songe wood *kifwebe* mask, Zaïre, height 12½in (31.7cm)
New York $159,500 (£94,940). 20.V.87

A Mahongwe wood reliquary figure,
Gabon, height 22½in (57cm)
London £28,600 ($47,762). 30.III.87

Opposite
A Baule wood mask, Ivory Coast,
height 17¾ (45cm)
London £14,300 ($23,452).
30.VI.87

Tlingit or Haida chief's ceremonial wood frontlet, north-west coast, height 7in (17.8cm)
New York $28,600 (£17,764). 27.V.87
From the collection of Marcia and Irwin Hersey

A Chimu silver male figure, *circa* 900–1250, length 8¼in (21cm)
New York $22,000 (£15,493). 24.XI.86

This figure probably formed part of a larger silver funerary assemblage.

A Fatimid rock crystal flask

Marian Wenzel

Historians of Islamic culture often dwell upon the opulence of the Fatimid period in Egypt, from the end of the tenth into the twelfth century. At this time the new city of Cairo was developing as a thriving centre for world trade. All manner of decorative silks were imported from Byzantium, Persia, Sicily and Spain; silver vessels were manufactured and exported to India; elaborate objects were produced combining gold, amber and pearls, and the lustrous effect of these materials was imitated in the humbler medium of painted pottery. Some of the greatest treasures of Islamic art were carved from rock crystal, applying a technique then at its height, a fine example of which was sold at Sotheby's in October 1986 (Fig. 1).

Fatimid art differs somewhat from the Islamic mainstream, a fact which probably reflects the unique position of the Fatimids as the most Africanized power to play a leading role in the earlier history of Islam. They were an Arab dynasty, originally centred in Tunisia, which they controlled with the backing of the indigenous Berbers. In 969 they conquered Egypt, and by the end of the tenth century held the whole of North Africa and much of the Near East, including Mecca itself. During the next century further links were made, both through trade and marriage, with black African areas, principally the Sudan. As a result of this diversity, Fatimid craftsmen seem to have combined their unparalleled access to raw materials with a design instinct that drew on Byzantine, Persian, Coptic and various African traditions. Their art is typified by a bold compositional approach, where strongly constructed design units, filled with fluid and often closely compacted motifs, are balanced by areas left free of decoration. This quality can be recognized on Cairo architecture of the period, as well as on ivories and textiles from Egypt and other regions subject to Fatimid influence.

Within this bold structural concept, works of art often display a naturalism absent from most other Islamic design of the tenth and eleventh centuries. For instance, animals and birds often appear, identifiable by type. Another outstanding feature is the obvious desire to obtain opulent effects by arranging surfaces which respond well, either by means of lustre, or of relief, to the play of light upon them. This is clearly the case with the rock crystal vessels: as lamps they would have flickered with gold light; as containers, the colour of the liquid would either have been intensified or would have emphasized the crystal relief.

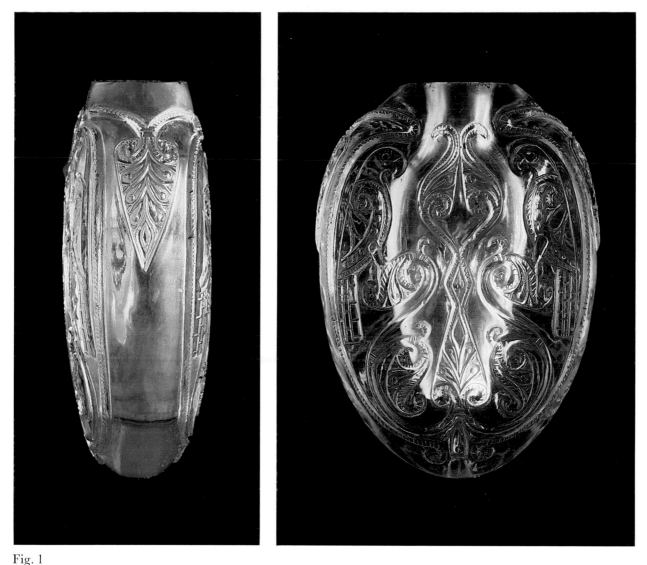

Fig. 1
Two views of a Fatimid rock crystal flask, late tenth–early eleventh century, height 4⅛in (10.5cm)
London £308,000 ($462,000). 15.X.86

Fig. 2
A Fatimid rock crystal ewer, late tenth–early eleventh century, height 8½in (21.5cm)
Reproduced courtesy of the Victoria & Albert Museum, London

The carved decoration of the flask sold at Sotheby's features paired birds, in this case parrots, which in Islamic symbolism signify the delights of Paradise, flanking upright palmette trees. It is a most important addition to the corpus of known Fatimid rock crystals, which at present numbers fewer than two hundred. The flattened ovoid shape is common to three others: one in the Freer Gallery of Art, Washington; another in the Victoria & Albert Museum, London and a third in the church of Santa Chiara, Assisi. All four have an axial arrangement of the chief design elements.

Since some of the most famous Egyptian rock crystal vessels have been preserved for centuries in European churches as reliquary containers, it is curious to reflect that some, at least, had a domestic use. Crystals were used not just by the Caliphs, whose magnificent collection provoked much wonder when plundered and dispersed in 1062, but also by well-to-do citizens of Fustāt and Cairo, outside the immediate court circles. Surviving trousseau and inventory lists from twelfth century Fustāt describe crystal vessels which were household items. When specified, they include a crystal mixing vessel (Arabic: *madāf*) for cosmetics and medicines, and a variety of crystal containers for the popular eye-makeup *kohl*, used by both women and men. A list from 1140 mentions a crystal mixing vessel and a crystal cockerel, presumably a storage vessel, the cockerel perforated and containing a *kohl* stick, which would have been a crystal or precious metal applicator. Two crystal *kohl* containers with gold rims are cited in a list from 1146, together with a mixing vessel. It seems quite probable that the flask under discussion was used to contain *kohl* and grinding at the lip suggests a fitting such as the gold rims of the crystal *kohl* flasks listed in 1146.

Kohl as worn in Egypt in recent centuries was prepared from a smoke-black composition made by burning frankincense and almond shells and, before the nineteenth century, had reputedly contained such admixtures as antimony as well as powdered gold, silver and pearls. Applied liberally by means of a rigid stick dipped into the diluted substance, it was felt to be highly beneficial to the eyes. Both *kohl* and henna were mixed with water for use. It is interesting to speculate that if flasks like the one sold at Sotheby's were used for *kohl*, crystal ewers such as the magnificent example in the treasury of St Mark's, Venice and another in the Victoria & Albert Museum, London, (Fig. 2) were used to add water to it in mixing bowls of the sort described in the twelfth century inventories.

The style of the present flask has been dated fairly securely to the closing years of the reign of the Fatimid Caliph al-Hakim (996–1021) or the early years of the reign of his son, the Caliph az-Zahir (1021–36). This date is also given to the two superb rock crystal ewers just mentioned. Stylistically they are close to the Sotheby's flask, in having notching to the edges of certain important motifs, a stroke and dot element to the leaves and square-cut edges to the relief carving. It is generally felt that these are workshop characteristics, which mark the climax of quality in Fatimid rock crystal production, and that after this period a decline set in.

Islamic art

A Seljuk whiteware cup, twelfth century, height 5⅜in (13.6cm)
New York $38,500 (£27,113). 24.XI.86

An Isnik pottery dish, *circa* 1530–50, diameter 11⅛in (28.2cm)
London £46,200 ($79,464). 16.IV.87

The only other complete example known of Isnik ware decorated with this unusual black and
white colour scheme is in the Victoria & Albert Museum, London.

An Ottoman steel helmet inlaid
with silver, *circa* 1500,
height 12in (30.5cm)
London £35,200 ($60,544).
16.IV.87

A Mughal silk rug, seventeenth century, 7ft 3in by 4ft 10in (221cm by 147cm)
London £19,800 ($35,056). 16.IV.87

A Lahore carpet, *circa* 1900, 14ft 8in by 14ft 6in (447cm by 442cm)
New York $49,500 (£30,368). 30.V.87

Opposite
A Tabriz silk rug, 6ft by 4ft 6in (184cm by 137cm)
London £26,400 ($39,600). 15.X.86

A Shirvan Marasali prayer rug, mid-nineteenth century, 3ft 8in by 3ft (111.8cm by 91.5cm)
New York $27,500 (£19,231). 13.XII.86
From the collection of the late Jerome Straka and Mary Jane Straka

A Mohtashem Kashan carpet, *circa* 1900, 9ft 10in by 6ft 11in (299.8cm by 211cm)
New York $35,200 (£24,615). 13.XII.86

Arms and armour

One of a pair of 12-bore *Royal self-opener* detachable sidelock ejector guns by
Holland & Holland, 1980
Gleneagles £29,700 ($46,629). 25.VIII.86

A 7.63mm M96 self-loading carbine by Mauser (Oberndorf) in a contemporary oak fitted case,
circa 1905
London £7,480 ($11,220). 16.XII.86

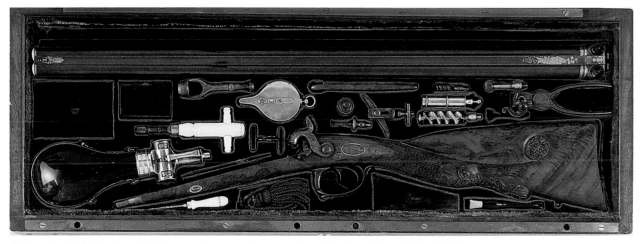

A Russian double-barrelled percussion sporting gun inscribed and dated *NT 1844*, in a
contemporary walnut fitted case, the lid with silver escutcheon engraved with the Imperial crest
London £9,900 ($16,236). 4.III.87

A pair of French tube-lock revolvers inscribed *Le Page arq^{er} du Roi*, numbered *1* and *2* and dated
1835, in a contemporary mahogany fitted case
London £21,000 ($34,440). 1.VII.87

Jean and Henri Le Page, father and son, are known for their many patents and adaptations of the
detonating system. These pistols, which appear to be based on the Collier patent, bear the cypher
of Ferdinand II of the Sicilies and are presumed to have been made for him. They are now in the
collection of the Royal Armouries, HM Tower of London.

Postage stamps

British Central Africa
(Nyasaland), 1894, a pen and
ink and watercolour essay
prepared by H.H. (later
Sir Harry) Johnston and
presented to Mr Buxton Forman,
secretary to the GPO in London
Johannesburg
R5,184 (£1,609: $2,335).
10.X.86

Great Britain, 1840 2d blue, an unused pair with full original gum
London £12,650 ($19,228). 2.X.86

Great Britain, 1866–68 pen and ink and watercolour illustrated envelope
addressed to Miss de Lisle, from a correspondence of sixteen such items
London £5,500 ($9,130). 2.IV.87

France, 1928, *Ile-de-France* cover addressed to Lieutenant Lablache-Combier, who was in charge
of the naval detachment aboard, which had replaced the civilian crew
London £2,145 ($3,260). 2.X.86

Collectors' sales

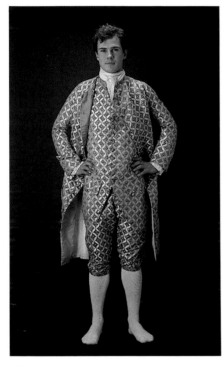

Above
A gentleman's brocaded silk summer
suit, probably French, *circa* 1760
London £13,750 ($24,338). 15.V.87

Right
The show-girl outfit worn by Marilyn
Monroe in the film *Bus Stop*, designed
by Travilla and bearing a woven 20th
Century Fox label, *circa* 1956
London £15,950 ($28,232). 15.V.87

An English embroidered
stumpwork picture
depicting the story of
Esther, *circa* 1660,
13½in by 17¼in
(34cm by 44cm)
London
£8,250 ($13,530).
14.VII.87

A Walt Disney celluloid
from *Pinocchio*, depicting
mechanical toys in
Geppetto's workshop,
1939, 9in by 11½in
(22.9cm by 29.2cm)
New York
$6,600 (£4,049). 27.VI.87

Above
A Hofner 'President' bass guitar belonging to Stuart Sutcliffe, a founder member of The Beatles, German, *circa* 1959–60
London £10,450 ($16,198). 28.VIII.86

Above, left
A universal double-crescent altitude dial by Johann Willebrand, signed, Augsburg, *circa* 1725, $3\frac{5}{8}$in by $3\frac{5}{8}$in (9.2cm by 9.2cm)
London £18,150 ($26,862). 28.X.86

Left
A gilt-brass mariner's astrolabe stamped *R 1602*, probably Portuguese, early seventeenth century, diameter $6\frac{7}{8}$in (17.5cm)
London £27,500 ($40,700). 28.X.87

Opposite
A German barrel orchestrion by Imhof & Muckle, *circa* 1880, height 9ft $11\frac{1}{2}$in (303cm)
London £39,600 ($63,360). 10.II.87

A German tinplate clockwork limousine by Marklin,
circa 1907, length 16½in (42cm)
London £18,700 ($29,920). 10.II.87

An American clockwork velocipede by Ives, late
nineteenth century, height 9½in (24cm)
New York $12,200 (£8,472). 16.XI.86

A German clockwork tinplate riverboat, *Maasdam* by Marklin, *circa* 1910,
length 19⅝in (50cm)
London £15,400 ($27,258). 15.V.87

Left
A French musical automaton of a bread seller by Leopold Lambert, the bisque
head by Jumeau impressed *203* and stamped *DEPOSE TETE JUMEAU 4*,
circa 1885, height 16½in (42cm)
London £12,100 ($21,417). 15.V.87

A French doll by Jumeau, the bisque head incised *10*,
height 22in (56cm)
New York $7,150 (£5,000). 16.XII.86

A French musical automaton of a banjo player
by Gustave Vichy, late nineteenth century,
height 20in (50.9cm)
New York $4,125 (£2,531). 27.VI.87

The Kay Desmonde Collection

Kay Desmonde

Today, child psychologists could explain why an unhappy child found it necessary to hoard secret treasures, but immediately after the end of the first world war the feelings of a sensitive child were of little importance to parents finding the struggle to rebuild a happy relationship just too difficult. I was not a child deprived of material possessions, rather the opposite. I had dolls, a rocking horse, mechanical toys and a beautiful mahogany dolls' house, a copy of my grandfather's Georgian home, made for me by my father from obsolete large rectangular toilet seats, seasoned wood being very difficult to obtain after the war. I carefully furnished this house over a period of about four years. My charitable mother could never understand the distress caused when periodically she removed my toys and gave them to the 'poor children' in the convent opposite our home.

Before I was ten years old I had realized that there was no hope of keeping my larger toys and had started to hide away tiny treasures. The first collection I can remember consisted of tiny cheap glass perfume bottles in animal shapes and, from this small beginning, an obsession with collecting the tiniest copies of artifacts of all kinds was formed. In later years, I replaced the dolls and toys I had loved as a child, and I also bought an early Victorian dolls' house, the furnishing of which was the spark to collecting on a much wider scale. I became preoccupied with Victorian childhood and this led to a lifelong interest and study, not only of dolls and toys, but of Victorian paintings, especially those featuring children with their toys, children's books, early postcards and porcelain figures of children.

Thirty years ago it was easy to buy examples of most items that would have been found in a Victorian nursery. At Sotheby's Bond Street furniture auctions I had virtually no opposition when a few dolls, always in superb condition, began to appear. Before I completed my collection I wrote two books (published in 1971 and in 1973), and from then on prices began to escalate. Sales specializing in dolls and toys were now held by all the major auction houses. Dolls, which had been the Cinderellas of collectable antiques, were accepted, and prices have now risen to unbelievable heights, as my William and Mary wood doll demonstrated (Fig. 1).

I became fascinated by the infinite variety produced by the different doll manufacturers, particularly by Gebrüder Heubach, one of the largest makers of dolls in Germany. Their main factory was at Lichte in Thuringia where the

Fig. 1
An English William and Mary wood doll, *circa* 1690, height 14½in (37cm)
London £67,100 ($112,728). 24.III.87
Now in the Musée Dina Vierny, Paris.

character faced dolls' heads for which this company is renowned were made. Over many years I collected forty-eight dolls, all with entirely different faces and some, particularly the one depicting a child having a temper tantrum, would have had limited appeal to children, but it is of course these rarer character dolls that are keenly sought by collectors today. Having decided to specialize in dolls made by Heubach, I went on to collect the bisque baby figures, sometimes called Piano Babies and also the Snow Babies, used for Christmas cake decorations. I limited my collection to fifty of each, but could have doubled this number without duplication.

My love of Steiff dolls was engendered by their whimsical expressions and aided by the fact that they were much easier to obtain (Fig. 2). Margarete Steiff, who was born in 1847, had polio as a child, which left her crippled. To amuse herself she made stuffed felt animals. From this very small beginning developed the Steiff Company, which is still one of the largest producers of toys in the Federal Republic of Germany. Her first factory was at Giengen in Würtemburg and here were produced the soft, huggable bears that were to be beloved of children right up to this day. Steiff's trade mark, a button in the ear, was originally introduced in 1903, and it seems surprising that so many dolls and bears still carry this tag as I would have thought that most children would have removed such a defacing object. During the first half of this century nearly every child would have had a teddy bear and a golliwog and, sadly, only the bear survives, but the dearly loved golly, with its large beak nose is now eagerly collected.

I collected examples from all the famous French doll makers: Bru, Steiner, Schmitt, Gaultier, Jumeau, Rohmer; beautiful dolls, whose superb quality has never been surpassed and represent the *crème de la crème* for collectors. But it is the miniature dolls, exquisite examples of the dollmakers' art, that have given me most pleasure. Those made specifically for dolls' houses I have often found too beautiful to hide in the depths of a Victorian dolls' house, so mine are usually displayed outside. I think I have proved with my collection of miniature items that the range is as vast as that of normal sized objects, and the detail often far superior (Fig. 3).

My collection, which had originally been for private enjoyment only, was occasionally exhibited for charitable causes when it gave so much pleasure that the idea was formed to open a small museum, in order to share the collection with a wider public. Thirteen years ago my first museum was opened at Syon Park, where it was enthusiastically received. Unfortunately, after only six years, the coach house where the collection was housed was needed for the expanding garden centre and a new location had to be found. Lady Ashcombe kindly offered part of Sudeley Castle in Gloucestershire and it was in this lovely setting that my collection spent its final years. It was with great sadness that the decision was made to close the museum at the end of last season, due to the increasingly difficult task of caring for it. Members of Sotheby's staff had shown interest in my toy museum from the early days at Syon Park, so naturally I turned to them for help and advice. Now, some weeks after the sale, I am hoping that my beloved possessions have found appreciative and caring homes.

Fig. 2
Left
A German felt doll by Steiff, with Steiff
buttons decorating his waistcoat,
circa 1915, height 13in (33cm)
London £1,870 ($3,142). 24.III.87

Right
A German felt doll by Steiff, with a Steiff
button in his ear, *circa* 1908,
height 16⅛in (41cm)
London £2,310 ($3,881). 24.III.87

Fig. 3
An English painted and glazed shop front,
circa 1940, width 60¼in (153cm)
London £1,980 ($3,326). 24.III.87

A 1925 Bugatti Type 35 supercharged Grand Prix two-seater
London (Honourable Artillery Company) £170,500 ($257,455). 1.XII.86

A *circa* 1934 Triumph Dolomite straight-eight supercharged two-litre open sports car
London (Honourable Artillery Company) £165,000 ($249,150). 1.XII.86

Opposite
A 1933 Alfa Romeo 8C 2300
supercharged cabriolet, with
coachwork by Figoni
Monte Carlo FF2,775,000
(£277,500:$462,500). 24.V.87

Right
A 1936 Buick 37.8hp DA90
'Limited' Limousine, with
coachwork by McLaughlin of
Oshawa, Canada
London (Honourable Artillery
Company) £143,000 ($233,090)
22.VI.87

This car was built to the order
of the Prince of Wales, later
Edward VIII.

Wine

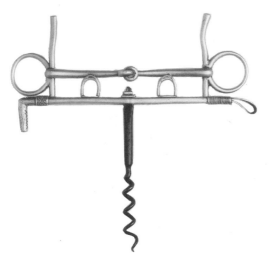

Left to right
A silver rider's corkscrew by Hamilton & Inches,
Edinburgh, *circa* 1890–1900
London £682 ($1,153). 8.IV.87

Château Margaux 1959, CB (two magnums)
London £462 ($702). 24.IX.86

Vougeot, 'Le Prieuré' 1961, OB (one double magnum)
London £209 ($318). 24.IX.86

For the second consecutive year the fine wine market has been somewhat erratic but London auction sales have held up well and have even reached new heights for the finest and rarest wines. The strongest demand has come from Britain and Europe, although private American clients have remained active and the Far East continues to grow in importance. Overseas, sales have achieved the best ever results in Tokyo, Johannesburg and Geneva. In the latter location rare vintages of Château Mouton Rothschild continued to attract attention and a new record for a bottle of the much sought after 1946 vintage was established at the 11 May sale at SF8,250 (£3,381:$5,612).

The policy of having fewer but bigger and better sales has been well received. For the first time Sotheby's sold more than half a million pounds ($865,000) of wine in one day at the outstandingly successful sale on the 3 June 1987, in which the highlights were sixteen bottles of old vintage Château Lafite, which realized £14,300 ($24,739), and an extensive range of Tokaji, including the fabulous Essence, which came direct from the Hungarian State Cellars.

The season started well with the inclusion in the first two sales, which took place in September and October, of the magnificent cellar of mature vintage port,

Left to right
Cognac, Grande Champagne 1789, OB (one bottle), London £2,200 ($3,718). 8.IV.87
Tokaji Aszú Essencia 1915, OB (one half litre), London £198 ($343). 3.VI.87
Château Lafite 1874 (one bottle), London £2,420 ($4,187). 3.VI.87
Château Lafite 1887 (one bottle), London £1,540 ($2,664). 3.VI.87
Château Lafite 1898 (one bottle), London £880 ($1,522). 3.VI.87

champagne and German wines from Bodwenni Hall, Llanderfel. A unique range of mature vintage champagne, shipped directly from the various producers and specially disgorged for the September sale, also sold for impressive prices. Throughout the season, the success of certain categories has been notable; the increased demand for vintage cognac has been reflected in the prices, and the same holds good for the finest Havana cigars, especially pre-Castro stocks, mature Pomerols and for collectors' items. Château Petrus has remained the highest priced wine with the majority of even immature vintages fetching between £1,000 ($1,650) and £2,000 ($3,300) per case, with new records set for the 1971 and 1982 vintages, both at £2,860 ($4,719) per case.

In addition to the popular wine evenings held regularly at Sotheby's, the department has hosted important tastings of claret, first at the London Wine Trade Fair in May and then at Vinexpo in Bordeaux in June. A new development within the department has been the appointment of Mr Christopher Ross with responsibility for sales outside the auction house, which has promoted the successful handling of major trade stocks as well as improving the 'finders' service for private clients.

'The Glory of the Garden'

C.R.L. Fletcher and Rudyard Kipling, *A History of England*, 1911

Rosemary Verey

Each year at Christmas Sotheby's lends its rooms in Bond Street to sponsor an exhibition to raise funds towards a charitable trust. This past year it was the Royal Horticultural Society and a celebration of the English garden. Exhibits were lent by members of the Royal family, by botanic gardens and museums and by many private owners. Robin Herbert, President of the RHS, called it a 'unique exhibition of outstanding works of art and artifacts of horticultural interest'. How right he was.

Gathered chronologically into centuries, the catalogue gave a brief and illuminating history of each exhibit. One of the earliest and most beautiful was an illuminated manuscript on vellum from the workshop of Jean Bourdichon of Tours in the early sixteenth century, the borders scattered with naturalistic flowers. Among a myriad of prints, drawings and watercolours, the RHS lent a series of beautiful botanical illustrations including a delicate study of anemones by Pieter van Kouwenhoorn, and there were studies of fruit and flowers by Venetian, French, Italian and Dutch artists.

Examples of garden furniture and tools spanning the fifteenth to the twentieth century showed how little these implements have changed. Among the garden tools was an earthenware thumb pot for watering that I had read about in *The Gardeners' Labyrinth* of 1577: 'The common watering pot hath a narrow neck, big belly, somewhat large bottom, and full of little holes.' Many contemporary portraits of great gardeners had been assembled: Monsieur Beaumont of Levens Hall fame, *Gardener to King James 2 & to Col Js Grahme;* portraits by Sir Godfrey Kneller of Henry Wise, gardener to Queen Anne, and of John Evelyn, diarist, scholar and the most famous writer on gardening and planting during the latter half of the seventeenth century. Overlooking the main gallery (see opposite page) was the tremendous portrait by Benjamin West of Sir Joseph Banks (see also page 49).

Through a variety of splendid exhibits, the changing design and style of the English garden could be followed. The background of the portrait of a lady attributed to Marcus Gheeraerts, *circa* 1625, shows an elaborate formal garden, evidence of a Jacobean layout. Forty years on, the 1662 bird's eye view of Llanerch portraying a terraced plan and enclosed gardens is a topographical record without equal of English formal gardens around the time of the Restoration. Straight alleys, canals and topiary slowly gave way to the landscape garden, and later still Humphry Repton's influence brought back flowers around the house, developing a style concurrent with the theories of the Picturesque movement.

A view of the exhibition mounted in the main gallery at Sotheby's, showing on the end wall
Benjamin West's *Portrait of Joseph Banks*, flanked by a set of four views of Castle Howard in
Yorkshire, *circa* 1771–72 by William Marlow.
On the left is a George III marquetry commode attributed to John Cobb, *circa* 1770, and above it
A Prospect of Tottenham Park in the County of Wiltshire by John Harris the Younger, surrounded by
views of Chiswick House by Pieter Andreas Rysbrack, and other views of the house by George
Lambert with William Hogarth.
On the right, above a George I sofa and a pair of chairs attributed to William Haller, *circa* 1740,
are *Views of Hartwell House and Gardens, Buckinghamshire* by Balthasar Nebot, and other views of the
house in the style of Edward Haytley.
The silver in the foreground is from the eighteenth century.

John Loudon took up Repton's mantle and adapted his style to the changing
social circumstances inaugurated by the Industrial Revolution, developing what
he called a 'Gardenesque' approach to accommodate the requirements of millions
of suburban gardens. Gertrude Jekyll, in collaboration with Sir Edwin Lutyens,
was to take the style a stage further, developing a cottage garden tradition,
characteristic of many gardens today.

The exhibition drew more visitors than any staged hitherto, a clear reflection of
the interest in gardens past and present. The catalogue was reprinted, the rooms
were constantly full, often with people who never before had walked through the
doors of 34/35 New Bond Street. The occasion was an unqualified success.

Notes on contributors

Barbara Bryant is writing a monograph on George Frederic Watts, based in part on her Ph.D. thesis for Columbia University, New York. She has written exhibition catalogues, including *The Drawings of Sir George Hayter* (1982), and contributed to the William Blake Trust's publication of *The Illustrations of the Book of Job* (1987). More recently, she has been a visiting fellow at the Yale Center for British Art.

George Daniels is a consultant to Sotheby's, a past Master of the Worshipful Company of Clockmakers and a past President of the British Horological Institute. He is also a watchmaker and specializes in developing precision watches. As a horological historian, he has contributed to a number of books and is the author of *English and American Watches* (1967); *The Art of Breguet* (2nd ed., 1978) and *Watchmaking* (2nd ed., 1984).

Philip J.C. Dark is an anthropologist, specializing in ethnic art, a subject that he has researched and taught in the United States and in Britain. His publications include *An Introduction to Benin Art and Technology* (1973); *Kilenge Art and Life: A look at a New Guinea People* (1974) and three parts of a thirty-two part study, *An Illustrated Catalogue of Benin Art* (1982).

Kay Desmonde has been an ardent collector of miniature items and toys for over sixty years. She has lectured, written numerous articles and published two books on the subject of antique dolls (1971, 1973), both translated into French, German and later Japanese.

Ann Garrould is Keeper of drawings and tapestries at the Henry Moore Foundation. She has contributed to many catalogues of Moore's work around the world including the Leeds catalogue *Henry Moore: Early Carvings 1920–1940* (1982); the Columbus (Ohio) Museum of Art catalogue *Henry Moore: The Reclining Figure* (1984), and has written on Henry Moore's drawings for a touring exhibition in East Germany. Her book on Moore's drawings is forthcoming.

Rüdiger Joppien is curator at the Museum für Kunst und Gewerbe, Hamburg. Together with Professor Bernard Smith, of the University of Melbourne, he has published *The Art of Captain Cook's Voyages*, 3 vols (1985–87). Rüdiger Joppien also specializes in the work of the artist Philipp Jakob de Loutherbourg.

Robert Rosenblum is Professor of Fine Arts at New York University and at its Institute of Fine Arts. He has taught and lectured at Princeton, Yale and Columbia and was Slade Professor of Fine Art at Oxford University in 1972. His many publications include *Ingres* (1969); *Modern Painting and the Northern Romantic Tradition* (1978) and *Art of the Nineteenth Century* (1984), with H.W. Janson.

Archer St Clair is Professor of Art History at Rutgers University, New Jersey. She specializes in late Antique and early Christian art and is currently working on a corpus of pyxides from this period. She has contributed articles on ivory pyxides to various journals.

Rosemary Verey is on the Council of the Garden History Society. She writes regularly for *Country Life* and is co-editor of *The Englishwoman's Garden* (1980), *The Englishman's Garden* (1982), *The American Woman's Garden* (1984), and *The New Englishwoman's Garden* (1987), and is the author of *The Scented Garden* (1981), and *Classic Garden Design* (1984). Also forthcoming is *The Garden in Winter*.

Dr Saul S. Weinberg is Professor Emeritus of Art History and Archaeology at the University of Missouri, Columbia and is Director Emeritus of the Museum of Art and Archaeology there. He contributed the chapter on 'The Stone Age in the Aegean' in *Cambridge Ancient History* (2nd ed., 1965) and is the author of several articles on neolithic figurines from that area. He has carried out excavations in Greece, Cyprus and Israel.

Dr Marian Wenzel has held a number of research fellowships and has taught in several universities, but now works as a freelance researcher and consultant. She has written several books and articles, chiefly on topics concerning the art and archaeology of medieval Bosnia, and early Islamic decorated glassware. Dr Wenzel's current researches concern the links between East and West in the decorative arts of the middle ages.

The following contributors are experts at Sotheby's:
London Julian Barran; Richard Camber; Roy Davids; Dr Stephen Roe; Julian Thompson.
New York Leslie Keno; Lucy Mitchell-Innes.
Geneva Nicholas Rayner.

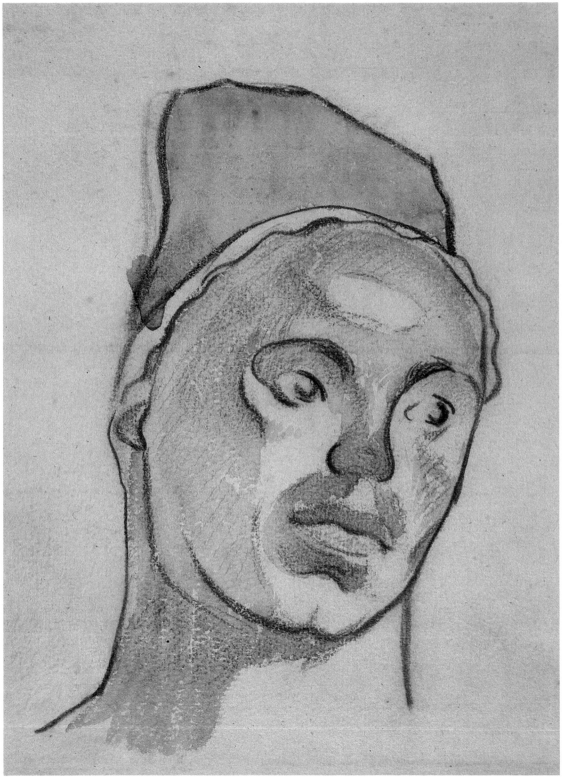

Paul Gauguin
ETUDE DE TETE DE FEMME BRETONNE
Charcoal and watercolour, *circa* 1894, 10¼in by 7½in (26cm by 19cm)
London £49,500 ($78,705). 19.II.87
From the collection of the late Sir John and Lady Witt

Index

A painted wood 'Dapper Dan'
trade sign, Philadelphia or
Washington DC, *circa* 1880,
overall height 77¼in (196.5cm)
New York $258,500 (£183,333).
25.X.86
From the collection of Don and
Faye Walters

A Tiffany Favrile paperweight glass
floriform vase, *circa* 1903,
height 15in (38cm)
New York $34,100 (£20,667). 12.VI.87

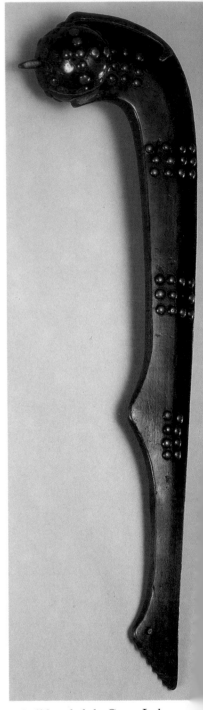

A ball head club, Great Lakes,
length 24¼in (61.5cm)
New York $22,000 (£13,665).
27.V.87
From the collection of Mr and
Mrs Rex Arrowsmith